PROPERTY MANAGEMENT GUIDE

ANDREW DUNCAN

ISBN: 978-1-5262-0166-9

First published in 2016

CONTENTS

INTRODUCTION

Welcome to the *Property Management Guide*, which is designed to help all landlords, property investors, and tenants. The area of property is already profusely written about, although existing books tend to focus on the end benefits of owning or renting property—buying and selling at the best prices, seeing great returns, and making sure you occupy on the right basis.

These are quite rightly the reasons for owning or renting property, but there is often little application of how this is supposed to work out in reality.

Why You Need Good Property Management

The mistake I see time and time again is owners and occupiers not realising that they need to proactively manage their properties. It's actually very simple and logical, but it often gets missed, maybe in the frenzy of focusing on prices and rents and the 'deal', and maybe because it's just not known or is too confusing. This has gotten better over the last few years due to the recession and the returns not automatically being there and therefore people need to look more closely at issues with their building and 'work the asset'; however, it's still so easily missed.

Compare this to buying or renting a car. You'll have an idea of the sort of car you want, the make and model, and maybe even the colour and spec you like. You'll hopefully look around at what the right market prices are and then make sure you choose the best possible vehicle at the right price. We all know the possibility of buying a bad car though—one that seems to have endless problems and costs afterwards.

We therefore make sure it's got a current MOT, a full service history, and maybe even a warranty and initial check over. We may even want our own trusted friend or mechanic to first inspect so we have peace of mind. And this applies to when you're renting a vehicle as well or when buying a new vehicle—checking what you're getting and making sure you don't get any nasty surprises afterwards.

So why don't we act like this with property? In fact, we should be even more aware with property as it's such a costly and more permanent purchase or rent as we're dealing with big figures. We therefore need to know the ins and outs of a property to make sure things go well.

Quite rightly the focus will be on the end result and the right property in the right location and the right price for you as well as simply having that feel-good factor. But understanding the true situation and making sure you effectively manage it going forward is critical to ensure that you don't mess up and get hit with all kinds of uncertain costs and issues afterwards. Just like buying a car that you discover needs a new clutch and major engine works three months after you purchase it, so with property you need to make sure you know what you're owning or renting.

The Full Perspective

So this *Property Management Guide* is designed to do just that—to guide you through the issues of owning or renting property to make sure you truly get the best deal. And the sooner, the better—many people turn to this kind of advice afterwards when they have an issue, but if you go through this before you even sign a lease or sale contract, then you go in open eyed and, in fact, can often negotiate a better price or rent in the first place.

It's been common in the bad market of the last few years for purchasers of property to 'chip' the proposed sale price down, not only by the market rates generally but also by coming up with a range of issues and problems that they have identified with the property that they quite rightly want reflected off the initial purchase price or rent.

The Author

My name is Andrew Duncan, and I'm a qualified surveyor who has been involved in managing both commercial and residential property for over 15 years. That's included all different kinds of properties, from individual houses, to flats above shops, to larger and luxurious apartment blocks. With commercial property, it's ranged from parades of retail shops, to office blocks and industrial estates, to unusual period buildings.

I've also helped a wide range of different clients, from individuals and properties held within their pension funds, to larger property companies and international institutions, to local-based management companies. This has included occupiers and tenants of buildings, whether individuals in their homes, small businesses, or larger retail chains across the UK.

All Residential and Commercial Property in the UK

This guide is designed for all kinds of property in the UK but focussed on England; there can be variations to consider for Scotland, Wales, and Northern Ireland. Also, the same principles can easily apply to other countries with careful reapplication within their own unique culture and legal system.

These are also similar principles for both residential and commercial business premises, but they just need a slightly different application in the detail. On the residential side, there are two main differences to be constantly aware of. The first is that there is more legislation covering property management as opposed to commercial business premises, the focus quite rightly being to protect people's homes and living accommodations. The second is whether you're dealing with short-term residential lets, say on Assured Shorthold Tenancies (AST), or long-term leases, which will imply greater ownership and rights for the residential owner.

This guide is therefore designed as a general reference for everything, with clear explanations of how it needs to be adapted for any variations in a particular property.

The Lettings and the Sales

There are two main types of transactions of property interests: firstly, a sale of the freehold or long-leasehold interest and, secondly, a letting with a landlord and tenant relationship in place (there are, of course, other variations of these and others). Good property management is needed in both scenarios, whether actually occupied by the owner or someone else. These are therefore all reflected in this guide, although there is more of a focus on the landlord's and tenant's situation as this often requires greater property management input and will naturally include any owner-occupier issues as well.

The Three People This Will Benefit

In terms of who will benefit from this book, I've got three types of people in mind. The first person is a landlord who is letting out their property to someone, and the second one is a property investor who is looking for a set return from the asset. Often both are the same person, with an investor needing to be a landlord and let out for an income stream, but these can be different, for example, if you own your own home or business premises and simply need to let it out to someone for a short time while you're away rather than become an investor for the long term.

The third is a tenant, someone who simply occupies a property on a temporary basis. The terms of this are often dictated by the agent or landlord, and they're left to sign the standard agreement and pay the 'set rent'. Well, here's the opportunity to read between the lines and make sure you agree to things correctly right from the start.

So the idea is that each section of this book has these three clear angles at the end so that you can easily apply it to your situation. There are also other points of view to consider as well, and, of course, this is still good material for other people involved in property, for example, a property managing agent or an insurance or mortgage interest.

See the Bigger Picture

Managing a property can feel like you're spinning lots of plates at the same time, or put another way, you have your finger in lots of pies. There are all kinds of things to remember and sort out, and often you're trying your best to make sure everything is 'spinning' and ticking along okay all at the same time. The bad news is that this is your job as a tenant, landlord, or investor in property; it's your property interest and your call to make sure it happens right. Of course you need others and professionals to assist you, but they're just there to do their literal job, and you often have to think between the lines a little and help make sure these different areas complement each other.

If you take a simple example of seeing a property in your local town that you want to buy, you decide to instruct a solicitor to deal with the legal side of the purchase and a surveyor to carry out a full survey to detect any problems.

a surveyor, solicitor, valuer, or mortgage company. You then have other third-party interests, whether other tenants and occupiers or your next door neighbours. Understanding these people and the rules surrounding their interests, including for yourself, is critical to then start seeing how each person plays a part in your property.

3. **Payments.** This is what the property interest will often boil down to: the money and payments between people. If you're a property investor or landlord, then you'll want to see a good price paid and return given for your property; after all, it's there as an investment and not just a building to look pretty and use. If you occupy property, then you'll of course want to see the costs of running your property reduced, the main one being rent, but all the other costs that have a habit of cropping up out of the blue as well.

4. **Paperwork.** The final step is the paperwork that documents everything that should be happening at the property, which can include all of the above three areas and issues to do with the actual property, people, and payments. It will also include the law of the land and what you need to legally do at the property, and therefore it goes wider than just literal paperwork but all other kinds of rules and documentation.

Although a lot of issues do in fact cross over all these perspectives, I've tried to keep them in the main and logical one but with reference to others where applicable.

The order of these four perspectives is also important to know as I'd say this is the natural order to think of them in. You start off with the literal bricks-and-mortar building, which is what it's all about, and then end with all the paperwork that helps document what this property is all about.

The Principles

There are a total of 53 principles outlined in this guide, which are the main subject areas within property management. They've been split between the four perspectives, although as above there will be some overlap between the various perspectives. So as an example, the principles of notices being sent is in the paperwork perspective as it's essential to get these documented correctly, although it is part of the whole communication principle within the people perspective and also referenced in other issues, about, say, leases and due monies, elsewhere in this guide.

Key Points

Within each of these 53 principles, there are various points to be made about that principle. These are in the general narrative on that principle, with key points summarised right at the start and then organised throughout the rest of that principle.

It's important to note that these are my pieces of advice in that area to help you out by being as clear cut and bigger picture as possible. If I was discussing with you face to face, these are the sort of points I'd particularly want to communicate to help you and won't necessarily be theoretical or say procedural steps taken out of a textbook. As above, you can always go into greater detail on one of these key points later; this is your helpful overall guide.

The Right Path

Sometimes it is helpful to have a more definite plan and checklist of what exactly you need to do in your own situation as well as how to assemble these all together in order to achieve your own personal goals. We are therefore developing various paths that can be followed for certain scenarios, a sort of route to logically and easily apply all the information in this Property Management Guide.

As an example, you may be a seasoned residential property investor purchasing your first commercial property or a new residential landlord with a small apartment to rent out, or you are looking to rent and occupy a new property in your local town; there will therefore be a more unique path through the four perspectives for your situation.

These are deliberately called paths rather than, say, a plan or checklist because of the idea that it is still a journey with different considerations en route that are dependent upon so many variables and choices to be made. They also make use of traffic-light style summaries, a principle I have used with clients over the years as a simple way to report on property management issues in a red/orange/green format to identify the urgency and priority of each issue.

What I have not done, though, is include these paths in this Property Management Guide book, simply because they need to remain flexible and be regularly updated; however, these are easily accessed through our website, www.propertymanagementguide.co.uk/bookpurchase.

Further Help

As mentioned above, there will be points where you need further help as the focus of this book is to be a guide to direct you through the complicated world of property management. At these points, we have mentioned any important points or phrases to research further as well as people and organisations to specifically contact for further help. Researching the things outlined, both on and off line, and contacting any points of help we mention will help guide you further through that particular issue.

We also have a supporting website, which offers regular blogs and updates on important issues within the property management world. Building up your general knowledge on the subject over time will help you not only on particular subjects in question but will also help you start joining the dots together and seeing how all these issues do in fact relate to each other.

The website includes a regular email newsletter for anyone interested; however, as a purchaser of this Property Management Guide, we can offer you much more, both general and more in-depth issues and updates but also additional material, such as the paths mentioned above, which will help support what you have learnt from this book. Go to www.propertymanagementguide. co.uk/bookpurchase for more information.

In the meantime, let's get straight into these key points by looking through the various four perspectives from the three different people interests in property.

THE PROPERTY PERSPECTIVE

1. Repairs

Key Points: Looking at the physical condition of the property and what repairs are needed is one of the most obvious and important property issues. Here are the key points you'll need to consider:

- *Have a proper look everywhere*
- *Go beyond cosmetic issues*
- *Gain an independent view*
- *Spot things, and then take action*

Have a Proper Look Everywhere

This is an obvious issue to look at. What is the condition of the property that you are purchasing, letting, or occupying? Have a good rummage around everywhere, and closely look at the property, in all the hidden parts if possible, like the basement or cellar, any loft or roof space (although being careful to safely access it), any cupboards under stairs or hidden in the bathroom or kitchen, and any outbuildings and garden areas.

Once you're involved with a property, whether as a landlord/tenant, owner/occupier, or managing agent, it's important to also have a system in place to regularly inspect the property to notice any issues early on, both general use or neighbour issues or repairs. Keep these well documented and communicated to relevant parties as well.

Go Beyond Cosmetic Issues

Also focus on things beyond just cosmetic issues, such as the state of decorations and quality of materials. This includes potential cracks in walls and things looking wonky, signs of wood rot or damp, any hidden items, such as a close look at the condition of the roof from outside and if there are any missing tiles or blocked gutters, and even the drains and grates dotted around. Ideally, you should do this with someone else who knows what they are looking for, like a building surveyor.

Gain an Independent View

If you're mortgaging the property, the mortgage company will probably send a valuer around, who should pick up on any main issues, but really a more detailed building survey under your direct instruction will really help you get to the bottom of any issues. If this can't be afforded or arranged, then ask a friend or someone you know to look at. An independent set of eyes will help when they aren't as emotionally attached to the property and situation as you are, or take lots of photos on your camera phone to show or email someone afterwards to check over.

Spot Things, and Then Take Action

Often common sense prevails, but it's up to you to spot and clarify it. So if you see something that it not right, maybe ask the other side to have it checked or surveyed more closely, or agree to a discount to the rent or price to reflect the uncertainty. You can also agree to have changes to any sale and lease documents that clarify these sort of changes in the negotiations.

Top Tip: Dealing with issues early on can save you time and cost later. Simple things like clearing roof gutters, making sure sufficient ventilation is in the property, clearing garden areas back, and basic redecoration of woodwork and fences can save you bigger costs and issues months and even years ahead.

When finding a surveyor to help carry out a full condition survey, as well as going on people's recommendations, make sure they are suitably qualified; for example, contact an organisation like the Royal Institution of Chartered Surveyors (RICS) to find a suitably qualified Chartered Surveyor in your area to carry out a full condition survey.

Landlord Focus: Check what the condition is and what repairs you may need to make directly once you bring in the paperwork perspective. Some of the 'hidden' repairs may need doing and paying for once you have a tenant and lease in place that you might not otherwise bother about. Focus also on what repairs and more cosmetic work will be needed to first attract and then keep tenants as it's easy to just look at through your own personal perspective.

Investor Focus: The condition of the property and subsequent repairs will have an effect on your investment value and return. Even if it's not fully reflected in any valuation, you may get hit with nasty costs and issues later on that you didn't budget for. This includes any longer-term issues such as regular redecorations or replacing rotten wooden parts as well as immediate issues.

Tenant Focus: Look closely at the condition, which may mean going back and revisiting after the first rushed viewing. This will help you spot things you will feel comfortable doing or what your landlord needs to be doing.

2. Alterations

Key Points: This links to the previous point about general repairs, although here's what you need to know from this alterations angle:

- *Find the new possibilities*
- *Establish what you'll be getting*

Find the New Possibilities

It's firstly about making changes, creating something different that can help a tenant better use the property or a landlord and investor derive further value. It's seeing the property through what-it-could-be eyes.

Look at what could be possible to improve the appearance, split or extend the area to increase the same or other uses and tenants, and add things to make it more usable. The paperwork perspective will affect just what you can do; there may be previous or new lease agreements, leases, licences of alterations, and inventories that will affect this, but at this stage, focus on just what could be physically possible at the property.

Establish What You'll Be Getting

Clarify exactly what you get with the property when you let or purchase it. The state that you see it in now may be different to when any transaction completes. There can be what they call chattels, fixtures, fittings, and furnishings at the property, which may not be intended or allowed to remain. There may be floor coverings, even false ceilings, shelving, both fixed and 'loose', and remnants left from previous occupiers, like counters, cupboards, kitchen and bathroom appliances, curtain rails and curtains and blinds, and lampshades. There can even be actual furniture, particularly larger, bulky items that no one has bothered to move, like beds and wardrobes and sofas, which can be costly for someone to remove afterwards.

Top Tip: Remember to check any outside garages, sheds, and out-buildings plus hidden areas like lofts and cupboards under stairs. There can be all kinds of things that have genuinely been forgotten by people.

I was once involved with a retailer desperately wanting additional space at the rear of a shop for storage and refuse bins who agreed to pay additional rent to the landlord, who was then willing to pay for a whole new extension to accommodate. This is a great example of alterations working for everyone: a happy tenant for more usable space and a landlord investor who had a profitable return on their further investment at the property.

Landlord Focus: Make sure things are resolved with any former tenant and that you have the area presentable for any new tenant. They may well be items you don't want, and it may be worth asking any future tenant if they would like them before removing. Think of alterations as well to increase rental value but also to tempt tenants to stay there longer.

Investor Focus: Watch out for costs of both carrying out new alterations and clearing up existing ones, which may hit your valuation or actual cash flow. On the up side, look at alterations that can increase the value of the property both in the short and long term, which can outweigh the initial or ongoing costs.

Tenant Focus: Be clear on the condition of the property and any former alterations that you want or don't want. Think then of how you want things to change, whether just minor bits and bobs or things that will involve major alterations to the property that you'll need to involve your landlord with.

3. Utilities

Key Points: They're so easily taken for granted but need careful checking out, so here are the key points:

- *Remember them all*
- *Suss out what's physically connected*
- *Find out their condition*
- *Work out the cost and hassle of new supplies*
- *Future energy savings*

Remember Them All

These include the basic supplies to the property: water, gas, and electricity. There's also Internet, phone lines, and TV aerials or dish connections, which have become almost just as necessary nowadays. We tend to take them all for granted, whereas they amount to a large running cost and can cause issues both with supplies and cables physically at the property and with accounts held with the utility companies.

Suss Out What's Physically Connected

One side to this is the physical connection at the property. You need to check what is actually supplied there and fish around to start understanding how this works in terms of where meters, fuse or distribution boards, or cables are within the property. Keep it simple, and start asking logical questions as to how this all works. Are there separate meters for each area that is able to be occupied, or are they shared? Are they easily accessible to take readings or carry out any repairs? Are there new meters, and are they the correct ones? So, for example, with electricity, you can look at day/night tariffs and then three-phase supply as an upgrade of supply and meters, which can catch people out.

Top Tip: If you want a gas or electricity meter moved to a better location in the property, be prepared for a long and costly process because the actual supplier will need to come and do this, not just an electrician or heating engineer. However, you can help with this by, for example, arranging any trench for new cables to be dug out already. Also, if you let, say, a corner shop out to baker, they may need a three-phase supply, which can cost thousands of pounds and cause delays for the landlord and tenant whilst being installed.

Find Out Their Condition

Check out the condition of cables and wires and these meter/board points. Okay, you're not an electrician, but just see if it looks old or new. You'll need current certificates by a qualified contractor to make sure these are certified and safe, and there can even be separate things like sub-stations and cupboards in hidden places that you need to be aware of.

Work Out the Cost and Hassle of New Supplies

If you need new supplies, then understand how this will work with the supplier, and don't get baffled by technical talk—things like are they installing at their cost, and how long will all this realistically take, and will they need to dig half the road up outside?

You'll need to see how all this is documented in terms of an account with a utility provider and ideally take copies of these so that when you're inspecting, then you can match the actual meters up and take current reads.

The key here is to appreciate that the company that you pay and have an account with won't necessarily be the actual provider, particularly with gas and electricity. So you may live in Scotland but have an account with Southern Electric. This means you can shop around and get the best rates from other suppliers by either contacting them directly or going through utility consultants. For larger properties, consumption, and business properties, you can also look at contracts with them to establish the best overall rates.

Make sure the account and charges match reality on site. Check that you're using the correct meters, the right readings, and the correct from and start dates. Be careful you're not sharing supply (and charges) with others at the property, as this may then need to involve separate recharges to people as often you can't get separate accounts with a utility provider even though you may have a separate sub-meter for them.

You'll also have to be careful with payments to the utility providers as they're hot on this. Miss these and they will charge you and threaten disconnection before you know it. They will want to have you on direct debit payments, which can make better rates, although be careful as they can suddenly take out of your bank whatever figure it is for that period.

For further help, you can do a lot of online searches for good utility rates and providers. Try to find good, clear, helpful guides from reputable sources. Utility advisors/consultants can help with bigger and more complicated issues, but be careful to get genuinely helpful ones—just ask around with others and real-life recommendations.

Top Tip: Always take a quick photo of a meter or meter area on your mobile phone; it's then easy to remember, and you can send it across to any utility company with any queries. This is particularly important when a new letting or sale completes.

In addition, a flat above a shop may have been built with just one set of meters as it was intended to be used by the same occupier, but now the flat has been refurbished with separate access from the front and a separate residential tenant. The landlord may need to still hold and pay utility accounts and then recharge the costs to the new shop and flat tenants rather than the cost and hassle of splitting meters. They could install a small sub meter to clarify an actual read in each area, but the account will have to stay the same; however, it also may be worth just all agreeing on a split rather than the cost and hassle of installing and taking actual reads from a sub meter.

Future Energy Savings

A final thought is the future. Energy saving and eco-friendly buildings are going to be more important with properties, and we'll see utility costs rise. It's good to look at other options, such as energy-saving measures to reduce utility costs generally, maybe even going wireless for your Internet and diverting your landline telephone numbers to your mobile so you don't even need a physical phone and Internet connection, and seeing what alternative energy sources are possible, such as solar panels on the roof.

Landlord Focus: Make sure utilities are easily split, they are changed for each tenant or shared area, and everything is certified and safe. Although you may not be responsible for their area, be helpful, particularly right at the start, so your tenant can be up and running easily.

Investor Focus: This sort of detail is often ignored, but you can get hit by issues through any eventual survey or issues later on, so look into it now. You may be able to pass responsibility on to tenants, utility companies, and previous owners.

Tenant Focus: Work out which utilities you need, and get specific answers from your landlord at the start about whether they're supplied and if you're lumbered with any existing utility accounts. A classic restriction in a residential flat lease is to not allow an outside satellite dish so you're forced to use any cable installations. You can also get around Internet line restrictions nowadays by using wireless technology and even using TV or phone requirements through an Internet connection.

4. Car Parking

Key Points: *Car parking is often far more important than what you first think, both in terms of practicality of using and how they are managed and charged for. Although it's a great idea for people to have and use cars less, in reality, an average household is still heavily reliant upon vehicles, often with multiple ones, and maybe unusual and larger vehicles for, say, work. They may also need to have visitor spaces. So here's the sort of things you need to be aware of:*

- *Look at options to have car parking*
- *Communicate and document the parking arrangements*
- *Make sure others still use areas of parking*
- *Try all options to easily resolve problems in a friendly manner*

Look at Options to Have Car Parking

Firstly, try to make sure they're available if you can as it will improve the usability and let ability of the property. As well as obvious locations like a drive or yard, look at other opportunities, like using adjacent or shared land, or even what parking is available on nearby roads and public carparks as existing spaces could be separately let out for an additional income stream.

Communicate and Document the Parking Arrangements

Secondly, make sure these are clearly communicated and documented. They are often best kept as just rights to use rather than within main lease demises as this practically helps control parking areas. There can be separate licence agreements, and you'll need to check if any other rights already exist with nearby occupiers, including within the land titles, and this will then all need to be clearly communicated to everyone that is affected by this so that everyone is in the loop.

As an example that I was involved with, a flat was being let out where the landlord requested that any new tenant not park on the access driveway at the front of this and other residential properties and suggested some other nearby locations. This was because they had agreed an extra rent from other adjacent flat tenants to park there instead. However, the tenant did a land registry search and discovered that the access road was not actually owned by this landlord, so they had no legal right to do this. The lesson—get your facts right, and be upfront with people to clearly explain, even if it's bad news.

Make Sure Others Still Use Areas of Parking

Thirdly, make sure they can practically still be used for other users. So if a flat is separately let above a row of shops with estate agents, the agents will probably be in and out of any shared carpark at the rear all day long and on Saturdays, and there may be problems with them jamming the residential tenants in. Also, make sure there is space for any emergency exit routes, being able to clean and grit any external areas, and collection of refuse bins.

Try All Options to Easily Resolve Problems in a Friendly Manner

The final point is to be ready for when things go wrong, both accidental and more deliberate. Always try the friendly option first; speak with other people directly to find out why this is happening, and look at agreeing upon a sensible solution. Maybe leave a note on the vehicle asking for them to contact you and first discuss. If the problem persists, parking-control measures can be considered, such as pop-up bollards in front of the spaces or a barrier for the area.

The final stage may be to instruct a carpark management firm to place fines on cars that are not allowed to be there. You often just need an upfront cost for legal signage and communication as these parking firms generate their income from the ticket fines (actual clamping of vehicles on private land is now illegal).

These firms can also help look at other ways to manage car parking areas to alleviate issues and even develop an income stream through issuing tickets, pay and display, and permits. Check that any carpark management firm is suitably authorised and part of a regulatory group like the British Parking Association. Still, carefully vet them out, though, and check off- and online reviews about them.

Landlord Focus: Clarify what spaces you can provide, and make sure this is reflected in your rent both with the main tenant or any separate carpark letting with another person. Clearly communicate this to everyone, and include helpful advice on where to park on nearby roads, etc., and the rules and regulations for using them, particularly with shared parking areas.

Investor Focus: Look out for additional income-generating opportunities for parking, whether on-going agreements directly or through a separate car parking firm that can manage a car parking area.

Tenant Focus: Get this straight even before you sign the lease—where any parking is, any restrictions, etc. Also make sure this is fairly reflected in the final rent you pay, and approach other nearby property or land owners to come to any separate parking agreements.

5. Rubbish

Key Points: A simple thing like removing rubbish can hopefully be straight forward once set up correctly but can cause big problems when it's not. Therefore, here's what to do to get it right:

- Arrange the right disposal
- Keep things clean and tidy
- Keep on top of extra rubbish
- COSHH and cleaning

Arrange the Right Disposal

For residential, you will be able to arrange for your local authority to collect free of charge, although with businesses, you'll need to arrange and pay for this yourself through your local authority or another supplier (check out discounts available for organisations like charities). Make sure you've ordered the correct number of bins to the right location and the most suitable times of collection in the week; private suppliers often refer to a 'lift' cost, which is one removal of one bin.

Shop around for the best rates, make sure they have the right documentation like a Waste Transfer Note, and check that you have a specific person to contact if for some reason they miss a collection or there are problems. Also clarify whether you need to purchase the bins, particularly with residential, through your local authority, although even after payment, they will still probably ultimately own them and will want them returned at some point.

Top Tip: Check if your building insurance has any requirements regarding refuse; they may say to keep it stored away from the main building in case it is set on fire and to have a lock on them or a general bin store area. These security measures can also stop others from using them.

Keep Things Clean and Tidy

Another point is to watch out for the hygiene of bin areas and that they don't start smelling, looking messy, and attracting rodents and flies. Make sure they're regularly swept and cleaned, consider a pest control company as well as a cleaner that can do, say, bait-boxes around here and the remaining outside parts of the property, and give them a thorough wash-out both inside and out as well as around the bins every so often.

Keep on Top of Extra Rubbish

There's also the issue of extra rubbish being generated and arranging for additional collections from the council, ordering skips for one-off clears, getting scrap dealers to collect any valuable metal items, and looking at alternative green/eco collection services. Search online, ask neighbours, and look at what else others in the area are doing.

Also watch out for fly tipping and people leaving things in shared areas. Try to nip this in the bud early—find out who the culprit is, and communicate through a sign or notice or direct contact. In more severe cases, you may need to look at CCTV cover, additional lighting, warning signage, and even security patrols to get on top of it.

Top Tip: The whole recycling aspect of refuse is getting bigger, and it's worth looking into existing refuse collection services to be able to do this through separate bins for different items, typical with residential, or sift the recycling parts out of the main bin back at the depot. Often there is no notable extra cost for arranging this, but it can take time and cause problems while everyone cottons on to any new way of disposing of refuse.

COSHH & Cleaning

On a related issue is the subject of cleaning, which of course generates waste in itself and goes further to make sure things are spick and span. The important aspect is to determine who is responsible for this and that it's carried out correctly. Remember, there tends to be additional responsibilities under legislation like Control of Substances Hazardous to Health (COSHH) to make sure there is no harm to people from, say, chemicals, slips, and accidents.

Make sure it's on top of and the right people are doing it rather than others having to step in or be at harm from issues; for example, used needles from drug users at the rear of a building, cleaning chemicals left around for children to tamper with, or solid floors mopped and not dried properly.

Landlord Focus: You may need to help arrange and control if there are lots of tenants and communal areas, although you should try to ensure that each tenant makes their own arrangements where possible. Clearly communicate this to them in a letter or 'tenant pack' with helpful local resources, including recycling, which is an important aspect for some tenants.

Investor Focus: Check to see if you're responsible for arranging and the costs involved, and make sure the building looks cleaner when you have other interests, like the insurers or prospective purchasers inspecting.

Tenant Focus: Ask your landlord before you even move in or sign up to a letting, even down to where the bins are stored and if they are even provided; otherwise, you could spend ages sorting and maybe paying for them afterwards.

6. Trees

Key Points: *Getting a handle on any nearby trees and large vegetation either on or adjacent to your property can save you from big issues later on, so here's what to look out for:*

- *Check nearby tree roots affecting buildings*
- *Watch out for overhanging branches*
- *Investigate the health of trees*
- *Establish any Tree Preservation Orders*

Check Nearby Tree Roots Affecting Buildings

Firstly, and probably the more common one that you often see on TV programmes about renovating property, is to see how close they are to buildings and if there are or will be issues with their roots affecting the structure and foundation. There may already be signs of cracks and subsidence or damaged drains, or they may be on the way. If you can't have a formal survey, then take photos and plot on a plan to ask for clarity later on.

Watch Out for Overhanging Branches

Secondly, as they grow, the leaves can bulk out, and branches overhang things. They maybe start leaning over the roof of a building, and the force of the branches disturb the roof covering, or the falling leaves can block gutters up. When they're in full leaf in the summer, that can act as a good barrier and natural screen of an area, which is why they are often used along boundaries to segregate off from other neighbouring areas. This filling out, though, can be a jungle and may need treating and clearing back to control and keep pruned and healthy. Although they are not the sort of areas that people should be wandering into, if you do get visitors or trespassers, then make sure overgrowth is not hiding a large drop or ditch that people could fall in.

In addition, you may have issues of trees and vegetation from your neighbour's land stretching over onto yours. Technically, these are still their responsibility, although you do have a right to reasonable pruning of parts over your area that are causing a nuisance. Communicate with them to see what you can get agreed.

Top Tip: Carrying out a special Tree Risk Assessment by a specialist in trees can help establish a record of the literal condition of large areas of trees and vegetation. Get them to consider any potential day-to-day issues as well, such as people loitering around these areas. As well as being helpful to identify problems and action points, they can help defend any problems and liabilities later on.

Investigate the Health of Trees

Thirdly, it's worth checking the health of these trees and vegetation to see that there is no fungus or dead parts that may need treatment or removing to stop further spread. One of the worst examples is Japanese Knotweed, which is a plant that has a root system that keeps on growing and causes serious damage, hence needing specific and legal ways to deal with it.

Establish Any Tree Preservation Orders

Fourthly, you'll need to check that no trees have Tree Preservation Orders on them, which means they are protected and you can't start changing or even necessarily pruning them without permission. They sometimes have a code number on them, and you can check with your local authority.

For further help, search online for 'tree preservation order', 'tree specialists', 'tree surgeons', or 'tree risk assessment'. Also quiz good local landscapers and gardeners of a good size, who should genuinely recommend local tree specialists and not presume they can do it themselves just for additional work.

Landlord Focus: Check what you are responsible for under the lease and what your tenant is; however, this is one of those major issues, which means even though it may technically be your tenant's responsibility, if the lease demise includes the whole rear garden for example, you'll need to clarify exactly what they are carrying out and come to an agreement on this. Focus on getting the basics right and understood, and liaise with the tenants to agree on any sensible ongoing maintenance.

Investor Focus: Although there can be advantages of an improved appearance and a natural barrier to your property, quite often you have to watch out for liabilities from them as above, whether roots, overhanging trees, or overgrown areas that are exposed to people. Surveys and risk assessments to document the true situation can help manage any issues that crop up in any sale and lettings but also any future claims; for example, neighbouring properties claiming that the roots of the trees on your land have damaged their buildings.

Tenant Focus: Makes sure you're not only clear what areas fall within your lease demise and therefore responsibility but that these are reasonable and you're not suddenly taking on all the bigger long-term issues.

7. Security

Key Points: Looking at how safe a property or piece of land is, is becoming more and more important; therefore, here are some main security issues to consider:

- *Assess the physical damage and issues*
- *Look at people's security*
- *Look at reactive security measures*
- *Look at proactive security measures*

Assess the Physical Damage and Issues

If there is a break-in or trespass on your land, then there are the obvious issues of any physical damage to the property and taking action to ensure any persons are off your property. You then have related parties to liaise with, including insurance companies to agree on pay-outs of any claim or parties such as the police, local authority, and neighbours.

In addition to obvious times and scenarios when the security of the property is at risk, such as night times and holidays when people are away, there's even normal living and trading times to consider, which can, in fact, be even more difficult to manage. So there may be a communal entrance area to an apartment block that has what they call a tradesman buzzer on the intercom so that anyone can get in during working hours.

As an example, when I was managing an industrial estate years ago, a couple of guys boldly walked on site in the middle of the day, ripped out metal pipework from some toilets, and walked off site with them over their shoulders, ready to be sold for scrap. This left water going everywhere, lots of building damage, and a complicated insurance claim to process.

Look at People's Security

You will also need to appreciate people's safety rather than just the property, which is actually more important. There may be a direct duty on you anyway to provide this for people, or it may be implied through legislation that includes even trespassers on your property, and you may just need to sit down with your landlord or tenant and work together on security measures that work effectively for the greater good of everyone and the property.

Look at Reactive Security Measures

Reactive security measures can include CCTV cameras and someone reacting to an incident on these cameras or a signal from an alarm going off to call the police. You can arrange for remote monitoring services to carry this out, being careful on their remit as there are quite rightly additional duties and training needed for people to deal with these situations. As an example, a receptionist in a communal area is not able to carry out security duties and confront people. You may have key-holders and a call-out drill to check things to make sure everything is correctly documented.

You also need to be aware of any compliance issues such as under the Data Protection Act 1998, Freedom of Information Act 2000, and Human Rights Act 1998 and registration with the Information Commissioner's Office (ICO) and SIA Registration. For businesses, a data controller and the right procedures and signs need to be in place. Domestic users don't fall within these specific obligations, although be careful if you have your own CCTV cameras pointing outside your flat and covering communal shared areas for example.

Another obvious reactive measure, of course, is an alarm that sounds, which can include an audible speaker on site by the remote monitoring company calling out and warning people. There can be flashing lights as well, and it's important to make sure the alarm is loud enough and maybe linked to someone to actually take action as, unfortunately, most people just ignore them if they are going off.

Make sure any external security firm is suitably qualified and authorised, and see if they are approved by the Security Industry Authority, which regulates the private security industry.

Look at Proactive Security Measures

In terms of proactive measures, then the main area is locks and making sure people cannot wander off. Think about how this is managed through keys or digi-codes or even fobs and more complicated access control systems. Also, how are these managed and reissued if people want more copies or have lost one, which can justify an additional charge for the hassle of arranging.

Landlord Focus: Think about how you want your property secured but also how you're going to make sure your tenant implements this and behaves, as any insurance claim will look at the actual situation and how it was dealt with.

Investor Focus: Security measures can improve both the letability and usability and therefore income of the investment as well as control costs of resolving any issues and high insurance premiums.

Tenant Focus: Understand what your landlord already has in place at the property and what your role is perceived to be. Keep in contact with your landlord, and let them know if anything is out of order. Even if this doesn't lead to anything, it shows your landlord that their property is in your trusted hands.

8. Using Space

Key Points: *As a final point in the property perspective, it's important to remember the space that you have with a property interest and the potential other uses this can have. It's the thinking-outside-of-the-box approach to property and seeing those hidden extras other than the main one at hand, which can help develop further income and value from the property as well as a direct benefit and use as an occupier.*

Here are a few ideas to get you thinking. It's important to mull these sorts of ideas over when you're actually there looking around the property and land and comparing against the surrounding area and opportunities. Take a step back, think almost instinctively, and, with common sense, let the ideas start to roll. You can then sift out the poor ones and fine-tune the better ones.

- *Telecoms equipment*
- *Internet and utilities*
- *Advertising space*
- *Unused space*
- *Double uses*
- *Splitting spaces*

Telecoms Equipment

This can fluctuate in popularity, but there can be the opportunity to place masts and dishes on buildings to help with local signals for, say, mobile phone operators. This can create a nice extra rental income, although it can affect the appearance of the building, and you will need specialist advice to ensure you find the best deal. Also, certain equipment has additional legal rights of occupation at a property beyond normal lease rights under a piece of legislation called the Telecommunications Act 1984.

Internet and Utilities

In addition to the standard services such as water, gas, electricity, and phone line, the Internet connection is also now a necessity through a variety of mediums, such as cable, wireless, and even radio waves to equipment on the top of buildings. This can not only help improve the marketability of your property with these good to go without the cost and delays to set up, but there can be opportunities to operate and manage moving forward, particularly in multi-occupied buildings and even for tenants with any neighbours or lodgers/sub-tenants. Examples include a monthly charge for wireless or hard-wire Internet provision, particularly high-speed for businesses, or arranging re-charges of gas or electricity through sub-meters with an appropriate management charge for time spent arranging this.

Advertising Space

Sides of properties are classics, or boundaries of land, to arrange separate advertising boards, signs, and agreements for income. Be careful of planning and neighbour implications though, and look at other options to get the best rates rather than simply accept the first offer that comes along.

Unused Space

There's often spare space around that no one is using or even aware of that can be usable space for tenants and rentable space for landlords and property investors. Examples include roof or loft spaces, outbuildings and garages, storage space under stairs or store cupboards, basements, any out buildings or land that could be separately erected, and any building extensions.

Double Uses

Think of opportunities where there could be a double use of the same space, for example, car parking spaces by different users during the day or night or storage space by someone and actual use space by another.

Splitting Spaces

A popular one over the last few years with the downturn in the market is making the most of any existing space that occupiers have. You could maybe split an area off and make multiple areas, which are then lettable to others, making sure access and services, etc., are correctly accounted for. As a landlord or property investor, you can plan ahead for this as additional revenue, or even as a tenant, you can look at subletting just part.

Landlord Focus: Whether you have an existing tenant or not to work with, think of other options to increase rental income, taking into account the cost of doing so. Discuss with local agents to make sure that any idea you have will actually have a realistic demand and income from it.

Investor Focus: Securing additional sources of income will improve your capital value and is worth looking at, again in context of any upfront or ongoing costs. Make sure there are no clashes with existing interests and that the end user has credibility. (As an example, you may be able to receive cash on a weekly basis for a local gardener to store goods somewhere, but that may be difficult to document and quantify into a serious income stream on paper to have an effect on your actual property value.)

Tenant Focus: Look at what space is included within your agreement and what you're probably paying for against what you actually need, both now but also if you implemented changes. See what space can be used by others, or maybe what the landlord wants back anyway, and be careful to check your lease or agreement as to what is permitted.

THE PEOPLE PERSPECTIVE

9. Landlord & Tenant Behaviour

Key Points: *The landlord and tenant relationship at a property is one of the most important ones that must be established and looked after correctly. Here's some of the general pointers to consider:*

- *Understand how reality matches the paperwork perspective*
- *Ensure clear communication*
- *Always keep calm*
- *Remember to have clarity*
- *Involve other representatives*

Understand How Reality Matches the Paperwork Perspective

In the paperwork perspective, there should be a contractual landlord and tenant relationship through a lease, licence, or other form of agreement, with specific roles stated in this document plus within other general legislation. A lot of this is covered in the paperwork perspective; however, in this people perspective, you need to remember that you are dealing with real people, not just a name on the paper.

So keep it simple. Treat others with respect and, as the old saying goes, how you would expect to be treated yourself. Even if you are looking at it just from a contract relationship, then this humanness will actually affect the issues, problems, costs, and hassle you can run into later on. This is particularly so with property where you have real people using a property as their home or business or meeting place, where often the smallest of niggly issues can grind on them and cause friction and bigger issues later on. And likewise, you have owners, investors, and landlords that have financial and contractual commitments that must be appreciated by occupiers.

Ensure Clear Communication

This is one simple principle to keep your landlord and tenant relationship on the right track. Keep an open and transparent dialogue with them, and update them on any situation, even if it seems trivial to you. Even if that repair or problem is taking time to sort, give them a quick text or email to let them know that; it will reassure them. When they first take occupation, have a clear 'Tenant Guide' about the property that goes through some of the day-to-day issues beyond the main lease agreement.

Top Tip: Think of what practical methods of communication will work best, and use them. It may be a notice board at the property, an email system, or even setting up a Facebook group or website. Even having a correct telephone number and email will help, although one word of caution is to keep away from the very pally 'I'm your friend in social media world', as the idea is to simply help communicate issues but still keep that landlord and tenant relationship rather than necessarily a friend perspective.

Always Keep Calm

This can be difficult to do, particularly when people are personally involved in the property. Emotions can run high, and tempers can easily be lost, and although you may have the sort of personality that will react first and think next, you really need to consider this, even if you need to involve someone else as an intermediary, like a letting agent or co-tenant.

One practical way to do this is to let the other side vent their frustrations. Let them chatter on and get it all out in the air, and just listen. Often they just need to know that someone has bothered to acknowledge the issue, and even if you then are honest and say that you can't actually deal with this issue in that way and that quickly, then often the way you've sympathetically dealt with them will mean they're okay with that.

Remember to Have Clarity

When you do liaise and communicate, make sure you're clear. Keep away from techy jargon, cut to the chase and get to the bottom line if you can, and come up with clear action and promises on both sides. So yes, you may have just discussed an issue with security and people loitering about, but you may need to be clear and therefore need to send a quick email to summarise what the issues are just in case the matter escalates and has to be reported to the police or insurers later on. Maybe the landlord has agreed to liaise with the friendly community police officer they know in the area to look out for trouble and the tenant to check with the neighbours to see if they have seen anything.

Involve Other Representatives

Think of how you can involve others in the landlord and tenant relationship, although you need to make sure these are purposeful and don't cause even more frustrations and issues. So a landlord or investor may decide to instruct a managing agent to be the point of contact, but you may still want to make initial contact to the tenant and be the point of contact for such things as repair issues, if you arrange these yourself, particularly in an emergency. Or as a tenant, you may want to involve other family members or business colleagues to deal with certain issues because they have more expertise in or for someone else making/receiving payments, a day-to-day contact at the property, or a person to speak with in the UK if the tenant actually spends a lot of time travelling and is not home that often.

I was once on the phone with a tenant of new business premises I'd just started managing with historic issues of service charge mismanagement. The previous owners had hidden away and not responded to answers, so I was left to now pick up the pieces and unravel the situation. They explained how the whole call was being recorded in case the matter had to be taken to court, so most of the call was simply sitting on the fence matter wise but in a nice way—listening to the issues, biting my tongue and keeping calm, promising to look into it and reply back in a specific time frame even if I didn't have all the answers by then, and dealing with some of the smaller issues that were within my power to easily fix.

Landlord Focus: Remember that you'll often be seen as the nasty landlord because of the perception of a landlord; therefore, show some humaneness and be clear on how you'll be dealing with issues, whether yourself or through agents or maybe other people or family within your business. Try to action some small things as this will communicate that you will do things when needed in the future and that it's not all talk.

Investor Focus: You need to carefully analyse the landlord and tenant relationships that already exist or are proposed and evaluate if these are going to cause issues and costs later on down the track. Try to speak with individuals, even just day-to-day chat as you walk around the property without them knowing who you are, and see what the general vibe is.

Tenant Focus: Get clarity right from the start about who the points of contact are for you but also the landlord going forward, including for different aspects like payments, repairs, and emergency issues. Try to come across as a helpful tenant who is genuinely looking after the landlord's property, and suddenly those otherwise niggly issues may become a priority for the landlord to resolve.

10. Occupiers Leaving

Key Points: *Having occupiers and tenants in a building is often the main goal of landlords and investors for income and occupiers in order to use a property; therefore, how and when they leave is an important subject. Whilst detail is explained in the paperwork perspective, here's a snapshot of some of the angles to consider with the actual people and interests involved at the property:*

- *Understand your objectives*
- *Understand the paperwork*
- *Negotiation*
- *Lease expiries*
- *Surrender*
- *Forfeiture*

Understand Your Objectives

What are you really trying to achieve? Maybe the problem you have is more the behaviour of the tenant or the landlord, which if resolved you're more than happy to continue in the property or with a tenant in. Have a check through the previous point about landlord and tenant behaviours, and see if you can come to some resolution because once you take into account the cost and hassle and time of trying to investigate and then find a new one or place, which may not even work out as well as this situation, then it may be best to try to work things through.

Sometimes, however, it can be worth ending things. Early signs may indicate that you need to deal with issues early on rather than escalate if you've tried everything else. Maybe the tenant is continually paying rent late or misbehaving despite endless promises. Maybe your landlord will not deal with any of those parking issues that you have a right to, and it's simply not working out.

Understand the Paperwork

If you do decide to leave or have your tenant leave, then first check the paperwork perspective and whatever agreement is in place. Without going into detail, see how permanent this is and what rights the other side have, whether a full-blown lease with rights to continue on at the property, even at the end of the official end date in the lease, or maybe a more informal licence agreement.

Negotiation

Then try to chat through with them. Even if things have escalated to not really speaking, still try, even if through written correspondence.

You can also go through others or use others in a bad/good cop situation. So if you're approaching your landlord then maybe get your spouse or partner to come from a different, friendlier angle, almost trying to be the peacemaker, and come to a fair settlement. Alternatively, you could use them as a reason (with their permission of course) for wanting this resolved and that they have started taking legal advice out of your hands. Therefore, is there any way to resolve this now?

Top Tip: Be careful what you do state in writing or even discuss verbally as this can be used in any future legal proceedings, sometimes even your own notes or private correspondence with your advisors in worst-case scenarios with rights like disclosure. If you do need to state things in writing, then clearly outline if this is something you do want 'off the record', maybe labelled 'subject to contract' or 'without prejudice'. At this stage, you'll need some professional help.

Lease Expiries

A natural time to see changes is when the lease comes to an official end. If this is straightforward and agreed upon, then still be clear on what's expected; for example, all rent to be paid to the end and the deposit returned afterwards as a separate issue without deducting off the final month's rent. Also clarify what condition the property is to be left in and whether the tenant is planning to do this themselves. If they are physically vacating before the official lease end, then practically, the landlord may want to have their contractors come in and freshen up with some new paint, but be careful that this is agreed in writing as the tenant still has rights until the end of the lease and the landlord could therefore be trespassing.

The most important issue, though, is the rights that can exist after this official agreement end date. There are rights under legislation for the tenant to stay on rather than a landlord being able to ensure they vacate straightaway. Notices may need serving beforehand to request this vacant possession, and the landlord will need to come up with good reasons for why they need to refuse any request for the tenant to renew their lease. These leases can 'hold over' while new ones have to be considered legally, which applies to business occupiers just as much as residential ones although under different legislation.

For further action, some solicitors, managing agents, or surveyors can offer a free review of your situation, or you can find information online through professional body guides and general searches.

Surrender

If the landlord and tenant want out, then you can just agree to surrender the lease (i.e., agree it ends earlier than it states). This makes sense, although this must be documented, ideally through a legal deed or document so that the other side cannot change their mind afterwards.

Forfeiture

A drastic measure is to look at the landlord forcing the lease to end earlier than it's due to naturally end even though the other side may not want this, but if they are misbehaving under the lease terms, then it can be implemented by what they call forfeiture.

You'll definitely need some help to get this stage right, not only making sure the correct steps are taken to ensure it is legally binding but being aware of any rights that tenants have for relief afterwards and reinstating the lease if they pay up or comply.

Landlord Focus: Leases ending will often become a priority when you have problems with your tenants, for example if they're misbehaving or they're not playing ball by agreeing to any sensible new lease and rental level. You'll need to suss out early on whether things can be resolved, and if not, look at the options to deal with while being fully aware of the costs and hassle that can be involved, particularly with a well-informed residential tenant who knows how to play the game and delay things for you.

Investor Focus: You'll want good-paying tenants in and not necessarily what they call vacant possession. In this case, check the soundness of these tenants for long-term sustainability, but also think outside of the box for any future plans of re-development or better or different occupiers and then the different ways you may then need to handle this and maybe different tenants longer term.

Tenant Focus: You're in a strong position with lots of legislation protecting you as well as your lease, so make sure you know what all these are, and don't be pressured into early action. Also understand what your landlord wants as it may help you to actually help them get another tenant in soon so they can agree to say surrender your lease early if you're looking to leave anyway.

11. Communication

Key Points: Communication between people is essential to make sure everyone's property interest is correctly understood and carried out, so here are three ingredients for successful communication in property management:

- *Establish proper communication*
- *When to limit communication*
- *Formal communication*

Establish Proper Communication

Suss out who you need to really get through to, whether a landlord or tenant or some other vested interest. See what the best contact is there, which is particularly important when it's a larger company that may have different offices, employees, and professionals like agents and solicitors acting for them.

Remember all the different types of issues you'll need to liaise with them on, and see if there are different people for each one. The three popular ones are an accounts contact, a day-to-day contact actually at the property, and a general correspondence address for formal notices or larger lease issues.

Finally, see what the best form of communication is, which often boils down to how they tick personally. Do they prefer speaking on the phone, meeting person to person, or communicating through emails and text messages?

When to Limit Communication

Sometimes you need to deliberately limit communication, particularly when you need to take a tough stance on an issue and play good cop/bad cop. So when a lease is coming to an end, on one side, you may want friendly feedback on whether the landlord will grant a new lease or a tenant will stay on, but you may have to stop formal communication as this may legally affect the way in which you can deal with issues, so you may have to rely on general feedback from others.

Formal Communication

After you have sussed out the best ways of communication and people to liaise with and you're well on your way to sorting everything out with them, always remember to then back things up in writing and some formalities as this can save you in the future when situations or individuals may change. It may be just a chatty and friendly 'hey, thanks for meeting earlier and clarifying this, that, and the other…', a more formal letter or notice through a solicitor, or even just a file note at your end.

Landlord Focus: Get your ducks lined up here, and know who the tenant is, who's actually going to be living or working in the property, how you contact the tenant for non-emergency and emergency issues, and some kind of back-up contact, such as business colleagues or next of kin.

Investor Focus: Focus not only on things going forward but what has happened in the past and any issues that have arisen with correspondence and documentation to prove this, including queries in any replies to enquiries through solicitors.

Tenant Focus: Make sure you demystify the whole process into who deals with what and how you get answers. Try to get a personal contact with the landlord or their closest representatives to get a feel for how they plan to carry out their landlord duties, and then determine what the formal and day-to-day contacts are, for example, a managing agent or through solicitors or their accountant.

12. Marketing

Key Points: Effective marketing of a property is essential for all tenants as well as landlords and investors to find and secure the right property interest, so here's what to remember:

- *Get the bottom line*
- *Involve others where needed*
- *Utilising the Internet*

Get the Bottom Line

This may sound so blatantly obvious, but it is so easily misunderstood and often missed. Firstly, get an understanding of what you really want, and in fact need, not what everyone else thinks you do. So, for example, is it a new tenant where you're willing to take a chance on them and a new business start or first home? Or do you want very temporary accommodation in the right area, and price isn't actually the main factor?

Secondly, make sure you get a reality check on this 'idea' by someone who does know the local market. So even if you're letting a property out yourself without an agent, still call some and sound them out to see what the market is actually dictating in terms of rents and sale prices being achieved and types of tenants/landlords or sellers/purchasers.

Involve Others Where Needed

Then start involving others, being clear on what you expect and their terms and conditions. The obvious help is some form of letting or sales agent, so carefully look into these and going on local recommendations. Maybe even look at appointing more than one on a clear joint agency basis.

Top Tip: This applies to more than just a landlord or investor wanting to let or buy a property. They may need assistance much earlier in the process to look at new purchase opportunities or market research into certain areas of town that should bring better returns, maybe near new up-and-coming areas. Also, for tenants, they could actually appoint their own agent or ask someone other than just the one acting for the landlord to advise with their best interests at heart.

Utilising the Internet

Don't forget the power of the Internet and the endless opportunities to check out properties across the whole world right now. But likewise, be wary that they are just giving you a snapshot, and local human knowledge in most cases is still worth seeking out.

Landlord Focus: If you're building up a portfolio, then it can be worth sticking with the same agent and source of information, although make sure you still keep them on their toes and back up with Internet or offline research of your own or from others.

Investor Focus: Make sure any advisors give you that longer-term investment advice, not just get-a-tenant-quick help. So it may be worth holding out while carrying out major works and seeking another type of occupier later on or even seeking them now and agreeing on a pre-let basis before you lift a finger with any building works.

Tenant Focus: As above, remember to take your own advice and research, and not just an agent's advice if they're acting for the landlord.

13. Professional Help

Key Points: Involving others will probably be needed at some stage, in which case this is what you need to consider:

- *Know your limits*
- *The three main areas*
- *Clarify the basis*

Know Your Limits

One of the greatest skills in managing property is knowing what roles you and others play. This boundary line will always exist somewhere, and although it will depend upon how involved and hands on you want to be with the property and people, it will still be there somewhere. Even with absolutely everything delegated out, you need to be the glue that holds everything together and make sure everyone has a part to play and does it well.

There will be areas of expertise where you will legally need someone else, for example a qualified valuer, or there may be areas where you may want to do some elements yourself, for example arranging all repairs, but using a managing agent to deal with the payments side and service charges.

Therefore, firstly know your limits legally, but then secondly know what limits you want to place on your own time and resources, and thirdly remember that you still need to do something, even if it's just linking everything together.

The Three Main Areas

There are three main areas of expertise to be aware of with your property management. The first is an obvious side, the legal side, mainly done through solicitors. Make sure they have access to all deeds and legal information for the whole property if possible, not just the task at hand, and that they have help understanding the practical property issues. As an example, they can help qualify what legal boundaries your land has on a plan, but you'll need to know if this matches reality and whether another physical boundary has been in existence over the years.

Top Tip: You can now download information on registered land titles and leases, along with plans, direct from the Land Registry website yourself for under £10. It may be worth initially doing this to look through yourself but then pass to solicitors to delve further into.

Secondly, there are property advisors, more on the purchase side, that will have an effect on how you manage property afterwards. This includes a valuer, whether your own or through your mortgage or finance company, insurance brokers, building surveyors, and letting and sales agents. The key here is to realise that they will offer important rational insights that you may not otherwise see, maybe because you're not as qualified or experienced as they are but also possibly because you are more emotionally involved than they are. They will help you take a good, sober look at everything right at the start, and although you need to make sure their advice is correctly dovetailed to what you need, it can be worth its weight in gold.

Thirdly, is more the property on the management side afterwards. The obvious ones are contractors and builders on the maintenance side but also others like risk assessors and managing agents and some of the initial purchase or letting ones like valuers and surveyors. The secret here is to realise when you do and don't need this help, as it's easy to default to somewhere in the middle and bumble along. So yes, there will be times when you need professional assistance on construction works, health and safety matters, or building issues, but once this is known and clarified, you could manage it yourself afterwards.

Clarify the Basis

Whoever it is doing whatever job you want, get it clarified. Firstly, do this in reality, face to face, and on site ideally, and thrash out exactly what you're getting for your money. Secondly, get it clarified in writing, with terms and conditions, contracts, evidence of their insurance cover, accreditation, and qualifications; and even just emails and file notes to back up what's been said.

Top Tip: When selecting a letting/sales/managing agent for a property, check that the firm is a member of an accreditation body and independent redress scheme, that they have a clients' money protection scheme in place, and that they have appropriate insurance in place, like public liability and professional indemnity insurance.

Landlord Focus: You're going to be tempted to have all kinds of professionals working for you, particularly if this is all new and confusing. Carefully sift through these to see what you really need, and then make sure you understand what you're getting for your money.

Investor Focus: Make sure all angles are covered, and bring in specialists where needed. It will then be critical to get all this backed up in writing so there are no loopholes in case anything does raise its head in the future, for example, when the property is valued.

Tenant Focus: Don't assume this is not for you, even though it will tend to be your landlord who has all these advisors involved. You could even have your own survey carried out and a surveyor helping source the right property for you, particularly for larger and more permanent situations.

14. Checks

Key Points: *You need to be aware of the different people involved and the various checks and accreditation this involves. The main ones are:*

- *Accreditation*
- *Suspected activity*
- *Immigration checks*
- *HMO*

Accreditation

Generally speaking, any kind of accreditation is more applicable for any external advisors, professionals, or contractors that are involved with a property; however, you can also have them directly for landlord and tenants. They will not only help you check to see that they are legitimate but also help raise their own profile and show integrity.

There are two things to bear in mind though. Firstly, check that they are actually part of the schemes they claim to be with by possibly calling the accreditation scheme or using search facilities on their websites. Secondly, understand when they are actually needed and not just a good idea. So maybe the building insurers insist that an electrician carrying out checks is with a certain trade body, or the mortgage company may require that the valuer has certain accreditation, whereas with landlords themselves, generally, they don't necessarily have to be accredited; it's just a good recommendation.

Suspected Activity

This can get confusing, but the main issue that you need to be aware of is potentially suspicious money changing hands in a transaction by someone whom you don't know, particularly when you're receiving cash. This includes obligations under the Money Laundering Regulations 2007, Terrorism Act 2000, and Proceeds of Crime Act 2002, with the gist of the anti-money laundering regime in the UK falling into two sectors.

Firstly, everyone must avoid any offence that includes the movement or possession of criminal property, and if an individual or business knows or suspects any transaction may involve criminal property, it can make an 'authorised disclosure' to the National Crime Agency (NCA) for consent to proceed with the transaction. Secondly, there are those with further duties because they do business in the money laundering 'regulated sector', for example estate agents and auctioneers, where they need registration with HMRC or another regulatory body, have checks in place, systems and controls, and training.

In terms of what identification and information you need, there are three main areas to consider. Firstly, have the ID of individuals or companies and trusts checked, including copies of photo ID such as their passport or drivers licence with a statement like 'I have seen the original document and certify that the photograph is a good likeness of [name]' and signed and dated by a suitable person, or copies of a utility bill in the last three months with proof of current home or business residence.

Secondly, have a reference and possibly a credit check on the person or entity. There are various agencies both on and off line that can do this. Ask around or search online, but be careful that you know what you actually receive from them and that you can provide them with enough information, such as previous addresses.

Thirdly, understand what you need to have in place to then deal with any suspicious activity or money.

Top Tip: Remember to actually gain the consent of any proposed tenant or other entity for carrying out a credit check or reference, and keep a written note of this.

Immigration Checks

There are new obligations under the Immigration Act 2014 that require residential landlords to check the immigration status of any proposed new adult occupiers. It is important to remember that the buck stops with the landlord, although their responsibility may be passed to any agent they appoint. Also, it concerns all adult occupation at the property, not just named tenants on an agreement, which means a greater awareness is needed of who is actually in a property on whatever basis.

Practically, within 28 days of a tenancy agreement, the landlord will need to establish whether the occupiers are British or European Economic Area or Swiss Nationals and whether they have a 'right to rent' with current immigration status and a right to live in the UK. This can be completed by checking original documents themselves or a right to rent notice from the landlord checking service at the Home Office website. Documentation must then be kept for at least a year after the agreement ends, and if they have a time-limited right, this must be checked again by the later of 12 months after the original check or before the relevant deadline.

HMO

The Housing Act 2004 details how residential buildings with multiple households are classed as a House in Multiple Occupation (HMO), which is licenced by the local authority (there is additional detail on what building this includes in terms of number of households and degree of self-containment and amenities). If a landlord manages a building without applying for this licence with the local authority, then large fines can be issued. The gist of this licence is to make sure the proposed licence holder and manager are proper and appropriate persons and that the property is reasonably suitable for occupation by the proposed number of people.

Landlord Focus: You will tend to be in the firing line with all the above, although with the accreditation side for yourself, this tends to only be a recommendation and not necessarily a legal requirement. Find helpful guides to give an overview and the bigger picture.

Investor Focus: Make sure these are correctly set up as any problems and discrepancies can be spotted in searches from any new tenant or purchaser. Deposits in particular will need clarity on who actually holds them and how this is accounted for in any transaction.

Tenant Focus: These tend to be more applicable to and arranged by the landlord, which can make it sound all very confusing; however, some may be applicable to you, particularly when you're involved with others like contractors and insurers, and, of course, your rent deposit. Swat up on this, then, through your own online searches and helpful tenant guides through government bodies and tenant associations/support, and don't be afraid to ask questions and probe your landlord and their agent for clear answers.

15. Trespassers & Visitors

Key Points: You will need to account for all other kinds of visitors to the property, including those that are uninvited, so here's what you need to remember:

- *Extent of liability*
- *Duties at the property*
- *Trespassers & squatters*
- *Travellers*
- *How to deal with visitors*

Extent of Liability

If you have invited visitors to your property, whether you have a specific friend calling around to see you by arrangement or you are allowing the postman to call in every day to deliver to you and your neighbouring flats, then there is a duty for the person in charge of different areas of the property to make sure everything is safe for them. That kind of makes sense, although the law actually goes one step further to say that it includes uninvited people as well, even trespassers and people breaking into your property. So although their entry on your property on one hand may be illegal, on the other hand, if you've got notable dangers that could harm them, then you can likewise be breaking the law yourself.

Duties at the Property

One of the main pieces of legislation is the Occupiers' Liability Act 1984 as well as other areas of law under Health & Safety, which provides this obligation for all kinds of 'visitors' to the property. The focus is making sure that things are safe, that there is no serious risk of say parts of the building falling down in a derelict building and hitting people, or holes in the ground that people could fall into.

It doesn't necessarily mean that you have to automatically solve these problems but rather manage them by maybe offering clear signage and instruction and control of persons around these 'dangers'.

Trespassers & Squatters

This is where you have uninvited people entering and then residing in your building or land, particularly those areas that are vacant. There was a notable change through the Legal Aid Sentencing and Punishment of Offenders Act 2012 making this a criminal offence for residential property, including just part of a property for residential, for example a flat above a shop. This means you can contact the police straightaway; in a similar way, to people coming in and stealing your TV, a criminal offence has been carried out.

For other properties, you're left to common-law and civil remedies. You, or preferably a certified instructed bailiff company, can use 'reasonable force' to remove them, which really boils down to asking them to leave. In most cases, this is unlikely, and you need to remember potential bailiff costs and the risk of a criminal offence yourself under the Criminal Law Act 1977 if at the time of eviction any person present on the premises is opposed to the eviction.

Alternatively, apply to court for a possession order to be served on the trespassers before a hearing for the court's bailiffs to then enforce. This can take weeks, although an Interim Possession Order (IPO) helps bring in a 24-hour timescale after which the police can take action, although often reluctantly.

Travellers

These are groups of people and small communities that see pieces of land to settle with vehicles and caravans, etc., for a period of time, often until they're forced out by the landowner or legal occupiers and authorities like the police, local authorities, and certified companies. This can become a serious issue for land and property owners, taking time and money and complications to effectively resolve, with three issues in particular to be aware of.

Firstly, take measures to prevent it from happening in the first place, listen for local feedback on potential Travellers or Gypsies in the area, keep prone areas like areas of grass with easy access from roads always inaccessible with fences, bollards, posts, etc., and, if needed, regular patrols and inspections and keeping the area well lit. Secondly, if it happens then go about things the right and legal way to begin the process of eviction, and speak with local authorities and sources of specialist advice, and avoid personal confrontation and allegations. Thirdly, when they do go, be prepared for any damage and mess left that will need rectifying.

How to Deal with Visitors

On one side, you need to be proactive and warn people as well as prepare a property so that it is suitable for people. You also need to be clear on how to react when things go wrong, so if there was an injury, are there any obligations to provide First Aid facilities or accident records, and have you checked that the 'visitor' does a lot of these checks and responsibilities themselves, for example a builder?

In addition, remember that even when you do have trespassers and break-ins, you can't necessarily act instinctively. You can't harm people, and you must make sure you can easily contact other authorities to go through the correct procedure of removal. As well as situations involving court action and liaising with the police directly, there are specific firms that will have experience in these matters to advise you accordingly.

Top Tip: Link this to the security issue in the earlier property perspective, and see what practical measures you can take to firstly deter this but then secondly pro-actively deal with afterwards in terms of alarms, call outs, or CCTV cover.

Landlord Focus: Firstly, check that any areas already let out to tenants have no liabilities back to you, the landlord. Although they, as the occupier, will have a lot of control over issues, you, as the landlord, particularly with residential, will still have obligations with more property-specific issues, such as the safety of the basic building and supplies like electricity and gas. Secondly, see if there are any areas of land you still own that are not demised to tenants, where you have full liability still, for example, shared communal areas, lobbies, and stairs or external grassed or carpark and drive areas.

Investor Focus: Carefully assess what liabilities the property owner has and then how they are being managed, including delegation and risk assessments, and making sure there is a paperwork trail to explain and support this.

Tenant Focus: Make sure the building is safe, and be clear on what aspects depend upon you as well as the landlord. Then assess how you actually use and control the space, including signage and access arrangements, levels of light cover, and then how you will effectively deal with emergencies by contacting others to help, etc.

16. Lease Names

Key Points: There can be a whole array of different names with a lease and therefore different people involved in the property interest. This is a popular document within property management and therefore the focus of this principle, however similar principles will apply to other property documentation such as deeds and sales agreements. Here are some of the main people and points to remember:

- *Establish correct names & contacts*
- *Joint names*
- *Guarantors*
- *Old and new tenants*
- *Subtenants*
- *Be wary of lease variations*
- *Understand the condition you're left with*
- *Help with practical matters*

Establish Correct Names & Contacts

The names on the lease need to form some kind of legal entity that take on the rights of the lease, the two popular ones being an individual's name or a company name, although there are variations of these, including partnerships, limited-liability structures, and charities. These are the 'people' on the line, so make sure these are what was intended and that they have the finances and ability to cover their duties under the lease.

For example, a local builder may want to take a lease on both new business premises and a flat to live in, and they want to put down their business name, "ABC Builders", on these two new leases. This is only a trading name, though, and simply for publicity purposes, with no legal entity; therefore, maybe look into the flat being in their individual name and the business premises being in the company name for the business, for example "ABC Builders (United Kingdom) Ltd".

Joint Names

You can have other names of individuals or even companies, which can bring peace of mind on both sides of the fence that another entity benefits from the lease but also has to pay the cost. However, although they are separate entities in reality, they are treated as one party for the lease, particularly for tenants, meaning that you can't suddenly take one off without any consequences. The lease may then need to end, or you will need to look at transferring the lease formally to just the person left.

Guarantors

This is where someone guarantees the obligations of the tenant in the lease, which includes everything, not just paying the rent and monies due. This can be a great way to add stability and security to a lease but still have just the original tenant on as the main party.

Old and New Tenants

If you want a new tenant to take over, then you're left with either agreeing with them to start a brand new lease or assigning the current lease over in writing. For former tenants, particularly with business leases, they can still be on the hook for any problems later on depending upon the age of the lease and any additional documents when previously assigned; you'll need to know what the procedure is to pursue these.

Subtenants

Maybe you keep the lease you have and just look to have a subtenant or lodger in to the whole or just part of the property. Problems can emerge though when you are still sharing the property and practical things like access and the rights across shared areas and services causing difficulties.

Be Wary of Lease Variations

Be careful when you make any kind of changes to the lease or take serious action under it as you may well need to inform and involve others like previous tenants and guarantors in order for these to be valid. Also watch out for changes when it comes to deposits and how these are used or transferred during or after a lease and involvement with other parties.

Understand the Condition You're Left With

One practical matter on this people perspective is to consider what the state of the lease and actual property is when you take it on. Know who's involved, what role they have, and how this will change, and see what the best way is to approach them to agree on anything—whether it's clarifying what the condition of the building is and whether any former tenant has to remove anything or if there are any former leases or separate obligations regarding deposits or rights that you need to consider.

Top Tip: Check who the previous occupier and tenant was and what the history is, and then get it confirmed in writing. If this is say a business tenant who apparently went bust three months ago and the landlord had to forfeit the lease, considering that they have a six-month buffer period of relief after to request their old lease to be reinstated if they pay these arrears off, then any new lease you start could clash with this and cause endless problems.

Help with Practical Matters

Get real practical, and think how you will be dealing with the property day to day when it comes to people and leases. Will you be getting lots of post addressed to a former tenant, and can this just be thrown away? Has there been a history of people involved at this property, including other tenants or even guarantors having to step in, and is it worth changing the locks and security codes? Also, what about any utility accounts and readings that need taking and changing over?

Top Tip: If you're moving into premises to occupy, look into setting up a post divert service with the post office to give it a few months at least for any old post to come straight to your new premises while you have time to tell everyone about your new address. Make sure you have the right person or company stated though, as anything addressed to another person or business name may slip through the net and end up at your old address.

Landlord Focus: Make sure you're not only clear on what the tenant name is taking the new lease, and if they're good for their money, but what they're really like on paper and in reality. Understand also any additional parties on the lease and how this will change things. Then make sure this is clarified retrospectively in any former leases so nothing can come back afterwards.

Investor Focus: Getting this right on paper is essential, which may take legal and property-professional help to determine how this then affects your investment value. So okay, it may be a great idea to let the property to ABC Builders because you know the chap and he'll pay rent every month, but on paper, the business is a new start and maybe adds no value to your property because it looks like you've just let it to a new company with no backing or history.

Tenant Focus: Check what you're getting on the lease or who was in there before to make sure you don't get any nasty surprises or visits. Think of how you can involve others if you're having difficulty in taking a lease in your name or company name because of poor credit history, maybe involving a guarantor or another tenant. Also, if the place is too big and costly for what you need now, is there any way to look at involving lodgers or subtenants to share this?

17. Disputes

Key Points: When you come across disputes with people and issues, here are three general ways of dealing with these:

- *Negotiation and conversation*
- *Formal dialogue*
- *Prescribed methods of dispute*

Negotiation and Conversation

First try everything to amicably resolve any issues and disputes. Let things cool down, involve others in the dialogue to keep unbiased, ideally try to meet face to face and on site, and be straight forward, as often you can resolve after any misunderstanding is unravelled or at least narrow down the contested issues. One word of caution though: if it escalates further, then be careful what you formally agree or state, particularly in writing, as this can he held against you later on.

Formal Dialogue

Secondly, start formulising this as the next stage. So maybe clearly state your position in writing, making sure it is 'without prejudice' or 'subject to contract' if need be and making sure it is correctly sent and received by them through any requirements in leases and legislation, for example, to be delivered by registered post.

It may also be worth instructing a solicitor to send a more direct letter, which will obviously have a cost to it, but this shows that you mean business, and it enables you to try to negotiate something on the back of this. Failing this, a process called Mediation is worth looking into, where each side has the opportunity to clearly state their case to a third party, who then provide advice on how this should be settled both in the perspective of being sensible and what's legal. Although it is not binding nor a definite legal decision, it can help give impartial decisions.

Prescribed Methods of Dispute

Thirdly, you may then need to 'go legal'. Before checking with solicitors though, just check what paperwork you have that may dictate how this happens; a contract with a contractor may determine adjudication as a specific means, a disputed rent review in a lease to go to arbitration or an independent expert, or residential rent arrears require particular notices being served.

Also, check what other methods of resolution exist other than involving solicitors, either described in any lease or contract or general legislation. So with long leasehold residential property, both the landlord and tenant should apply to the First-Tier Tribunal (Property Chambers), which was formerly the Leasehold Valuation Tribunal (LVT).

Landlord Focus: Try to determine straightaway if things can be easily resolved or if there is a pattern of issues emerging that are worth nipping in the bud now.

Investor Focus: Although you may not be directly involved with these things, be careful what you inherit and what issues are bubbling away that may crop up afterwards.

Tenant Focus: Know your rights and ability to peruse these, including with funding assistance, although realise your limits as you can get carried away, particularly with solicitors who, after all, still need paying no matter what the outcome, unless agreed otherwise.

18. Management Companies

Key Points: Management companies can be involved in property management; here are the main issues you'll need to be aware of about them:

- *Residential properties*
- *Freehold titles*
- *Managing agents*
- *Company matters*

Residential Properties

Management companies can exist in situations where the legal ownership and leases at a property are complicated, and therefore an intermediary company comes into play to help tidy things up. In principle, this can make sense but can end up being complicated in reality and difficult to unwind when you get involved with a new property.

So to keep things simple, there are two main areas where management companies are useful, the first being in residential properties where there are lots of different tenants or owners, for example a block of flats. These companies can help residents actually take control of day-to-day management of the communal shared areas like the stairs and lobby, away from the landlord.

For single blocks of flats, under the Landlord & Tenant Act 1987, long residential leaseholders can apply to a Tribunal to appoint a new manager because there is a problem with the current managing agent or landlord breaching obligations or being unreasonable. This is not actually involving a new 'management company' but just exercising a right to affect the way a landlord manages a property.

Under the Landlord & Tenant Act 1985, such long leaseholders can collectively apply to become a 'recognised tenants association' with statutory rights such as being consulted regarding any new managing agent as agreed together with the landlord or by the Tribunal, but again, no management company is yet being looked at.

The other method is the Right to Manage under the Commonhold & Leasehold Reform Act 2002, where tenants have the automatic right to take over the management of the shared areas so long as certain pre-requisites are met irrespective of whether the landlord wants this or not or is not at fault in any way. These must be self-contained flats with at least two long leases making up at least two-thirds of the flats in the property (other detailed requirements as well). Practically, notices are served, and a new company is set up to take on management duties and service charge collection and management, but the freeholder still collects any ground rent and deals with lease issues like re-entry and forfeiture.

Top Tip: If tenants are looking to take control of a shared property, it's worth looking at the freehold purchase as well, which will involve a management company anyway, although there will be a premium to pay. The tenants will end up with greater control, the ability to then vary leases and end ground rent charges, and may be able to improve the property's value.

A final option with residential property is for tenants to look at a shared commonhold interest at the property introduced under the Commonhold & Leasehold Reform Act 2002, which is technically not just a management company but a different form of ownership. In reality, though, this has not ended up being a popular option.

Freehold Titles

The second area is where you start involving separate freehold titles, and a management company may actually take ownership of a freehold piece of land, not just have a right over it. So you may have a small terrace of office units on the outskirts of town, where each unit is owned freehold by someone, but no one wants the hassle of taking on the communal carpark or landscaped area. So a management company is set up simply to hold the communal land that all the other unit-holders, who benefit from and contribute costs towards running, are part of.

Managing Agents

These are different to management companies in that they are instructed to carry out duties on behalf of the companies and are not the actual management company itself. So a management company, ABC Holdings Ltd., could be set up to hold communal land, and they decide that local estate agents XYZ Lettings & Management down the road actually deal with day-to-day matters, so the directors of the management company may decide to instruct XYZ to do this and pay their fees and charges through the management company.

Company Matters

These management companies are often just normal companies, so they are registered with Companies House, have certain legal and accounting obligations to submit accounts or tax returns, and have shares or membership of it and appointed directors or secretaries.

So on one side, you may have each flat tenant or unit owner having shares or membership within such a company and therefore having rights to vote on matters, hold AGMs, and appoint certain people to be directors with authority to agree on matters. There can be Articles of Association and Memorandums saying what the company does and how it is to be operated. On the other property-related side, there can be legal Deeds of Covenants or leases obliging each tenant or owner to benefit from the company and land and pay the company maintenance or service charge for doing so.

The important thing is to realise that these 'company matters' are separate to 'property matters'—with the former, it's all about membership and shares and obligations under company law. Under the latter, it's how any land or property rights that the company then holds relate practically to other leases and land.

Top Tip: When talking about accounts, the company ones can be separate and simply to do with the company and can infact be dormant (i.e., the company is not meant to make a profit, just tick things along, so everything they spend is charged, and there's no net activity in the basic statutory company accounts). If this is the case, ask for a more detailed service charge or income and expenditure reports or sub accounts, which can provide more detail beyond the statutory obligation on what has actually been spent and charged for these shared areas of land.

Landlord Focus: Understand if any management company already exists, not only with the tenants but with any adjacent land. If they do, then be clear on how these may affect how you run your property. Also, watch out for any future opportunities for others to request any new management companies, particularly with residential properties and tenants' rights.

Investor Focus: Similar to landlords, take care on what already exists and what may be requested, and although it may not affect you day to day, it can affect the value of different interests. The worst-case scenario is where your freehold could be taken away by a management company.

Tenant Focus: Check out the wider area or block and property interests linked with your landlord to see what already exists or what could exist. You may have rights to instigate new things, although you'll need to weigh up the cost and hassle of going through this process and getting others possibly on board as well.

THE PAYMENTS PERSPECTIVE

19. Rents

Key Points: *This is often the most important aspect of payments; therefore, here are some of the main points to remember in order to get the most from this:*

- *Get correctly stated*
- *Prepare payments*
- *Late payments*
- *Set-off*
- *Notices*

Get Correctly Stated

Check any existing lease or agreement to see how rent is described, and use the opportunity to shape any new documents. In most cases, it will be what it says on the tin, 'rent', which has legal implications with it. Sometimes, though, it can be a 'licence fee', which has fewer legal implications although in some circumstances still takes on the legal benefits of a rent.

You can also have a smaller and longer-term ground rent or peppercorn rent in longer leases, which although is often there just for the principle of a rent, these can still be worth charging and paying, to form a considerable rental stream. As an example, a lot of new apartment blocks will often have a ground rent for each flat lease of maybe £250 per annum, which may not sound like a lot, but in a block of say 10 flats, this totals £2,500 PA steady income for decades to come and therefore has a notable investment value.

Prepare Payments

The golden rule is that it's the lease that determines rent being due, with any accounting information like invoices, account statements, and reminder letters (apart from situations mentioned concerning notices) being a nicety rather than a necessity. These are helpful from a money-management side, but check your lease to be clear on what's due and when.

Top Tip: Sending accounting information like invoices, remittances, and summaries can more easily be done online nowadays through email or PDF copies or accounts on websites when you log in. There is an initial learning curve and cost to this, but it is worth looking into in order to benefit in the long term.

Practically, it's worth being clear how these monies are going to be paid. The textbook answer nowadays is via bank payments, maybe regular standing orders or direct debits, BACS payments, or urgent CHAPS payments. There's a clear record, and you can easily control it, often online. Cash may look more appealing, but you've got to cash it in and allocate it, plus there may be regulation issues of dealing with people's cash.

However if you are receiving cash, then provide a clear receipt and log for this, including a rent book and keeping a clear trail to be able to provide annual statements later on for tax purposes.

There's also cheques, although these are becoming less and less popular, plus there are delays in receiving them and then having them cleared in a bank account.

For residential property, if this has been permitted, then a landlord may need to help cooperate with a tenant's claim for local housing allowance/housing benefit/universal credit and provide any necessary information. If payments are missed or late and they're paid directly to the landlord, then immediately notify the tenant, or if they are paid to the tenant but the tenant's payment to the landlord changes, then inform the local housing authority or Department for Work & Pensions as soon as possible.

Top Tip: If you're looking at taking drastic action under the lease, such as forfeiture, these are times when you may not even demand or collect rent as this will be seen as acting as if everything is all okay under the lease. Get this clarified with legal advice, and be ready to deal with any payments that you still receive from a tenant or ones you want to still make to your landlord to try to stop any action.

Late Payments

Leases will often state the consequences of payment not being made, including interest being charged after a certain period, opportunities for the landlord to take action, and the tenant paying costs in pursuing these options. The important aspect here, though, is the point of formal receipt of payment to trigger these things, the emphasis often being on the landlord receiving the money rather than the tenant issuing. So even with a bank payment, it can take a few days to clear in the landlord's account, and obviously with cheques, there can be delays in receiving and cashing.

Also, check situations like lease renewals or break notices and whether you should or should not be formally receiving any rents in their entirety and even make formal arrangements to try to return it to the tenant.

Top Tip: In the initial lease, try to get as much practical detail in as possible, for example, what will happen when payment is not actually paid or received and even how payments need to be made (e.g., by regular standing order).

Set-off

For tenants, it can seem unfair to have to pay rent if your landlord has not been doing what they should be doing under the lease, particularly if you've had to step in and carry out and pay for an emergency repair yourself. It can be tempting to withhold rent or deduct, or 'set-off' an amount from the rent to account for this; however, check the lease as this if often specifically not allowed and means raising these issues with the landlord as a separate matter.

Notices

For residential long leasehold properties, the landlord needs to, by law, send a prescribed notice with the ground rent invoice as per The Landlord & Tenant (Notice of Rent) (England) Regulations 2004 (and similarly for service charges). Failing to do this can mean a tenant is not obliged to pay these charges.

Also, as a general point, it may be best to place phrases like "subject to contract" and "without prejudice" or send any invoices with a covering letter to clearly state the legal basis of any rent being demanded, for example when you have a lease renewal situation or outstanding rent review.

Landlord Focus: Rent is often the most important part of being a landlord, but don't miss the details in your eagerness to receive this. Get this clear in any situations like licences, temporary agreements, and lease ends, and send any notices and letters you need to. Also, try and get as much detail as possible in the original lease on how the money will be practically paid to you.

Investor Focus: This rental income is key to your investment value, and therefore you're often more bothered about what the amount is on paper rather than the practicalities of collection. But a poor payment history by a tenant can be eventually reflected in the valuation, and you may need to deal with any arrears being collected upon any sale and affecting the final completion price.

Tenant Focus: Remember that paying rent is the most important thing for your landlord, so the better you are at it, the better things will go for you generally and when dealing with the landlord on other issues. Keep it clear, regular, and prompt, and if you do come across payment difficulties, then nine times out of ten, being up front with your landlord will be the best way to come to a sensible agreement.

20. Arrears

Key Points: *This is when rents or other monies are not paid for whatever reason. Here are the main points to realise, with the detail of any specific procedures dealt with in the later paperwork perspective.*

- *Know the options*
- *Determine the root problem*
- *Costs of receiving*

Know the Options

Payments are 'in arrears' when money is owed by someone, usually rent not being paid in time to the landlord or other monies such as service charge or insurance premium. For landlords and investors, this can be a real problem; after all, rent is the bottom-line reward for letting the property interest, and for a tenant, it is a worry if these simply can't be paid for whatever reason and they suspect action being taken by the landlord.

Firstly, check what the procedure is for chasing and collecting these according to the lease and general property law. Is there a timetable for action being taken and when the landlord can start charging interest on payments? Often it doesn't prescribe how they can chase these, such as formal letters or emails or calls, although it's worth checking. When sending any letters of claim or letters before action, which is basically a warning about imminent legal proceedings, make sure this has the right criteria within it under the Practice Directions or Protocols under Civil Procedure Rules (CPR), particularly for residential property, which is where legal help can be beneficial.

The important thing will be any correct notices and procedures to undertake, particularly with residential property, which will require certain prescribed notices for shorter-term leases and also seeing if, in fact, there are times when you deliberately don't take action as this will prejudice any further action.

Secondly, look at other options before the ultimate action of involving solicitors and court proceedings. Check if there are any other forms of backup security, such as a rent deposit to use, or any guarantors or former tenants to call upon. With service charge arrears, for example, can the landlord reduce the services and therefore costs? If they're not receiving payment, they may need to still carry out legal services and facilities and comply with service charge legislation.

Top Tip: Remember other interests you may need to inform about the arrears, particularly any mortgagee, where you can check with sources like Land Registry as borrowers may be breaching the mortgage agreement if they breach their lease, although they're unlikely to agree to any debt settlement via the mortgage unless a court order or Tribunal determination is in place.

Determine the Root Problem

Try to get to the bottom of what the issue is. In a lot of cases, there is actually a good reason and a sensible solution, such as a delayed payment or payment plan. As a landlord, you need to discern this carefully as it can be a sign of poor payment history and intentions, and as a tenant, you need to have a reality check of being able to pay future as well as current charges.

Understand clearly whose name is on the line and if they're good for the money. Is it an individual, and are there signs of struggle in other areas of life or business? If in a company name, then is that company struggling and at risk of going into administration for example?

Costs of Receiving

Finally, understand what the total cost is in pursuing arrears, and check out the later paperwork perspective on some of the procedures. This will obviously include legal fees and correspondence, but also add up yours or others' time in this as well as normal credit-control procedures. Then see if any of these costs can be recovered through the lease or general legislation.

For further action, there is often a lot of information online or through helpful guides from solicitors or other support groups on how to pursue and collect arrears or how to pay and afford them as well as react to action taken to collect them. Check that it's applicable to your situation through taking into account whether it is residential or commercial property, the nature of the lease and tenant, and the amounts at stake. Try to get professional advice before any serious action, including any free consultations or help services.

Landlord Focus: This will be one of the biggest and most applicable issues for you, so make sure you try to nip any issues in the bud first while being clear on what the most effective way is to deal with it. Be careful, though, not to take it too far into your own hands, particularly if you get personally involved and frustrated and it's your money not being paid, as that may be the time for solicitors or others to get involved and take an impartial stance. They can also often play the 'bad cop' angle, and you can try to keep the friendlier open dialogue with the tenant for a practical solution.

Investor Focus: Determine the ability of your tenants on paper to be able to pay arrears as this can be reflected in your valuation and obviously cause cash flow issues if not being paid later on. Also watch out for any inherited arrears with new investment properties.

Tenant Focus: If you're struggling to pay your landlord, be careful on how you approach this before they take action, and don't be scared by threats. Often early dialogue with the landlord will help as well. Also, there may be circumstances when the landlord owes you money, which often has to be dealt with separately to your rent payments to them.

21. Rent Reviews

Key Points: *These are opportunities to change the rent which unfortunately can be easily misunderstood. Here's some of the main issues to be aware of:*

- *What determines them*
- *Alternative methods*
- *When you disagree*

What Determines Them

If your lease is several years long, then you can agree to have what they call a rent review clause and opportunity to adjust the rent during the lease term rather than just continue throughout. In most cases, the gist is that this should be to a fair market rental level, although a lot of leases, particularly business property leases, can have what they call an upwards-only rent review clause, which means that the rent can only go up and not reduce, even if the market level is genuinely below the current rent. This is to protect the landlord's and investor's income so that they know they have a guaranteed minimum level of income during the lease, although arguably this won't be fair to the tenant when rents are falling.

For residential long leaseholders, there is often a ground rent of up to a few hundred pounds a year, but carefully check how this may increase way in the future by steps of prescribed calculations.

First check the lease to see what it says about how such a new rent is calculated but also what the procedure is to agree it. Often it needs to be agreed after the new start date of the rent as you need to look at what the market level is at that point, but you then back-date any changes to this point along with any interest payments.

The basis of this 'market rent' will often be stated in the lease, or in general legislation, and with older regulated residential tenancies, there is a right to a 'fair rent'. You may need to assume all kinds of factors about the lease and property to make a theoretical market rent rather than what's happening in reality in an attempt to assume ideal market conditions. So you may need to assume a certain length of lease is being taken, that the whole property is empty with 'vacant possession' and all current fit out works removed, and unbiased tenants and landlords with no personal interests in the property.

Top Tip: Watch out for any old rent reviews in the lease and any additional documentation, such as memorandums, that these have already been agreed. Otherwise, they can suddenly crop up in the future with a liability or benefit to the landlord and tenant.

Alternative Methods

Look out for alternative ways of calculating new rents in any current leases as well as thinking outside the box for any new ones, particularly with business premises. These can include index-linked rent reviews, where the rent goes up in line with, say, RPI index in the general economy, or for more retail-based properties, they can be linked to the turnover and profitability of the actual store and will involve looking at detailed business accounts for the actual business.

Top Tip: Retail premises in particular get complicated with adjustments called 'zoning' and 'ITZA' rates to reflect space at the front of a shop area being more valuable. Take care and seek advice to understand and interpret this carefully.

When You Disagree

In most cases, you'll probably disagree with what the other side first suggests as a new rent. Even if you're both trying to be fair, a landlord will naturally want to be more optimistic with rents and gain the most, whereas a tenant will be less so as they explain the difficulty in living or trading. So don't be bullied into agreeing anything; do your own homework, and make sure you have a reality check.

Then try to logically and helpfully explain and negotiate with the other side before having to look at any further action described in your lease or general legislation which can involve appointing and using third parties to determine this, whether a court or authorities like an Arbitrator or Independent Expert. Be careful, though, on how this is done and what it will cost as someone will often need to pay the hefty bill going down this route as it ends up taking much longer than expected.

Landlord Focus: Do your research both in the lease and legislation but also the general market to see what the reality of any rental change is. You're going to be tempted to be over optimistic here as it's your money at stake, so listen to any helpful surveyors and local agents that can help provide a reality check of what the rent is or even the correct way to calculate it in the lease. For commercial business leases, you often have to break it down into a rate per square foot or metres of space and then adjust it for your particular property and circumstances.

Investor Focus: Look carefully at these rent review points, and determine if they can go up as well as down—and not only what you think any new future rents could be but how any individual tenant will react to this and want to take it further with third-party help and assistance.

Tenant Focus: Don't be bullied by the first proposal from your landlord. Do your own research, and see if, in fact, it can be reduced. Even though there may be a fair case to increase by, say, 10%, then see if the landlord will agree to reduce for your particular circumstances, for if you're a well-behaved and long-standing tenant, they may be open to this rather than stretching you to any point of payment difficulties.

22. Deposits

Key Points: Dealing with and holding deposits can be easily missed, which causes problems afterwards, so here's what to remember:

- *Types of deposits*
- *AST deposit registration*
- *Remember to use them*
- *Correctly hold them*

Types of Deposits

The most common one is rental deposits, particularly with shorter-term residential lettings, where it is the norm to take a month's or six weeks' rent to hold as a deposit until the end of the lease to act as a safety net for the landlord to use if there are any missed payments or the property is left in poor condition at the end.

Another is when you actually purchase a property with, say, a 10% deposit being paid at the start and the remaining monies paid at completion. Here the deposit is actually part of the full sale price, not a separate amount repaid afterwards.

You may also find them mentioned with third parties, such as contractors that require one before starting any works and buying materials.

AST Deposit Registration

For Assured Shorthold Tenancies, landlords are required by the Housing Act 2004 (and amended by the Localism Act 2011) to register their tenant's deposits with one of the authorised protection schemes, which basically means transferring the money to a third party to safely keep hold of it. There is then a set procedure for both the landlord and tenant to have it released at the end of the tenancy.

In terms of specific requirements, the landlord needs to issue prescribed information and tenancy deposit protection certificates to the tenant within 30 days of receipt, which can include older agreements that have since renewed and triggered this obligation for any original deposit, and any renewal AST or fixed-term AST that continues as a statutory periodic tenancy.

If a landlord gets this wrong, it can mean a claim to pay back to the tenant three times the amount of the deposit and can hinder any action a landlord wants to take against a tenant later on, such as serving a section 21 notice.

Top Tip: It's in the interests of both the landlord and tenant to get these types of deposits protected. You can find the main government-backed TDPs (Tenancy Deposit Scheme), issue payment to one of these and then issue both the prescribed information and certificate all within the time frame. Ideally, get your landlord or tenant to confirm in writing that all was processed and received okay, and remember to make sure any historic deposits are now protected.

Remember to Use Them

They're a neat little tool to use in property management. With rental deposits, if you have any concerns with any new tenant, then you could simply ask for a larger deposit to offer more security, or as a tenant, if you have a poor credit history, which means you get refused a letting, then actually offer an additional deposit to show the landlord you mean business.

Similarly, in any property transaction or instructions, they can be used to not only provide security for someone else to perform what they promise to do but make sure they finish the job or complete on a deal right to the bitter end. So if a contractor does major works, make sure a final deposit and retention is not returned until all works are satisfactory and snagging works completed.

Correctly Hold Them

Make sure you understand who actually holds the deposit money and then how this is documented. It may not always be the person like the landlord or investor who has these in their own bank accounts but rather their representatives like solicitors or managing agents (see above for special residential requirements). Then make sure the money is safe in a separate interest-bearing account and that it won't get absorbed with the landlord's other monies if they say go bankrupt themselves.

Landlord Focus: These are helpful to make sure the tenant is on the hook for obligations and payments under the lease, but make sure it's clear on how they are practically held, used, and documented as this can cause issues later on, particularly with residential properties, as failing to do this correctly can limit action against a tenant later on.

Investor Focus: Make sure these monies are clearly established during any property transaction, both in terms of purchase-deposits needing payment up front and the basis of these being returned if things fall through or get delayed and any rental deposits that need passing over.

Tenant Focus: As well as making sure you pay and have deposits held correctly, you may even want to offer additional deposits to sweeten your landlord or when you're involved with any building works for example. For residential properties, check that your landlord has gone through this correct procedure to hold and communicate this deposit so you have a right to request this back afterwards.

23. Service Charges

Key Points: *This is a huge area of property management to consider; here are some broad-brush points to consider:*

- *The basic principles*
- *The procedures*
- *Residential property*
- *The problems*

The Basic Principles

The idea is that they cover the cost of running any shared parts of a property, for example, communal corridors and stairs or external carparks and landscaping. As these can't be demised to particular tenants to look after directly, the landlord maintains control and responsibility for them with everyone then chipping in towards the cost of this.

It's usually accounted for every year, normally on an accrual and prepayment basis with allocation of debits (expenditure) and credits (income) to the period incurred or due rather than when paid or received, with every tenant or occupier of the building as a whole contributing towards this according to the degree of use and benefit they have of these shared areas. Usually this is based upon the area of each demise, so if tenant A has an occupied area twice the size of tenant B, then A will pay twice the service charge that B does in the apportionment. There are, however, other basis, for example, the number of bedrooms in each residential unit or carpark spaces or the rateable value of each area.

Top Tip: Get this basis of apportionment sorted straightaway as you draft any new lease, or check any existing one. They may not state this level of detail, and this often allows the landlord to have discretion to change the basis so long as it is 'reasonable'. You could also agree by side letter or turn to a reputable industry guide such as the RICS service charge codes for residential, commercial, and mixed-use property.

There are two other important service-charge principles to understand. Firstly, understand that the landlord needs to chip in as well in accordance to any vacant areas that don't yet have a tenant rather than simply spreading these costs out amongst those that are actually let or occupied. The principle is that it's based upon who has the right to use the shared services rather than who is actually there at the time.

The second point is that the types of costs in the service charge should generally mirror normal running costs and general repairs rather than extravagant improvements or extras. When these additional costs are needed, then there may be an additional procedure to go through to make sure they are legitimate charges.

The Procedures

Accounting-wise, there is often a budget set for the next accounting year in advance that breaks down what costs are expected to be incurred and how these are apportioned between all the tenants. Everyone then pays towards this during the year, often every month or three months in advance so there is money in advance to pay the bills from a separate service-charge pot of money away from rent or other monies.

Top Tip: Make sure any initial budgets are realistic and not just low forecasts to help, say, sell new developments by communicating low levels (also a potential breach of consumer protection legislation). Also, remember to clarify whether they include VAT or not, particularly with residential property where they need to be 'gross' VAT.

At the end of the year, the actual costs are totted up and maybe checked by an accountant, and any adjustment charge is raised in a final year-end 'reconciliation'. So if extra costs have been incurred above the original budget, an extra balancing charge will be raised, whereas if there is any underspend, then a credit will be issued and money credited back. For residential property, there will probably be an obligation under legislation as well as leases for these to be audited by an external accountant, who will prepare certain types of accounts such as balance sheets, whereas with commercial properties, it is often dictated by just the leases.

Top Tip: Both landlords and tenants need to be aware of any year-end reconciliations that haven't been accounted for yet. They can take a few months after the end date anyway to complete, but sometimes they can be years old. Make sure there are no nasty extra charges due one day, or on a positive note, see if there is any money due back. Even if money is due back, then it may be worth accounting for in a sinking or reserve fund to save for any future costs.

Leases should have a fairly lengthy service charge section that outlines the detail of how the service charges operate and lists specific types of costs to be included. Watch out for items that may be needed in the future and open-ended ones such as other general services to help the 'estate management' of the property, or any other security measures to manage the property.

Residential Property

Residential property does have specific legal protection concerning long leasehold interests under the Landlord & Tenant Act 1985 and Commonhold & Leasehold Reform Act 2002, which you'll need to be aware of.

Firstly, all service charge contributions received by landlords and managers (other than social landlords) are required by law to be seperately held monies on trust for leaseholders.

Secondly, check what party's costs are being paid through the service charge; so, for example, a landlord can't pass on their costs of any Tribuneral or court proceedings through the service charge as per section 20c of the Landlord & Tenant Act 1985.

Thirdly, there is a general obligation for service charges to be fair and reasonable, with either side able to apply to a Tribunal to determine what service charges are payable and, if need be, agree to any changes to the lease.

Fourthly, costs must be actually charged within 18 months of being incurred; otherwise, the tenant is not obliged to pay them. This initial point of occurrence is often when the landlord is liable to pay this cost. This can cause problems if, say, service charge accounts are delayed; however, if they are, it can still be due so long as the tenant is at least notified in writing before the 18-month time limit that these costs have been incurred and will require payment under the terms of the lease.

Fifthly, it's mandatory with residential long leases for the landlord to serve a notice with prescribed information along with each service charge demand to each tenant. This basically outlines and reminds the tenant about their rights and obligations regarding service charges and must be in the exact form as in the Service Charge (Summary of Rights & Obligations, and Transitional Provision) (England) Regulations 2007 . In addition, demands must confirm the name and address of the landlord, and where not UK-based, an address in England or Wales to serve any notices to the landlord.

Number six, tenants can request a summary of service charge costs under section 21 of the Landlord & Tenant Act 1985. Therefore, in reality, a landlord will need to supply service charge details within a month of receiving such a notice or within six months of the accounting year end as per point four above, whichever is later, and if the building has more than four units, these will need certification by a qualified accountant.

After receiving these details, the tenant can then serve a section 22 notice within six months to actually inspect and take copies of accounts, receipts, and other documents, to be provided free of charge by the landlord. Under section 23, the landlord must pass these section 21 and 22 notices on to any superior landlords to comply with, and any previous owner landlord who is still responsible for the period in question under their ownership.

Number seven, under section 30a of the Landlord & Tenant Act 1985, leaseholders can request a summary of the insurance cover, where the premium is paid through the service charge, and inspect, take copies, or have sent by post or ready for collection as necessary, to be provided free of charge by the landlord.

Number eight, there is a set procedure to notify tenants of any larger service charge expenditure, both one-off and ongoing contracts, under section 20 of the Landlord & Tenant Act 1985 (as amended by the Commonhold & Leasehold Reform Act 2002). Such 'qualifying works' must cost each leaseholder more than £250 or ongoing 'qualifying long-term agreements' more than £100 per accounting year; therefore, if the procedure isn't satisfied for these, then they will be unrecoverable from the service charge (a Tribuneral will look at the landlord acting reasonably in any emergencies). Interestingly, any agreement entered into before the building is constructed or let will not be part of these obligations. The detailed procedure is in The Service Charges (Consultation Requirements) Regulations 2003 but basically consists of a series of notices being sent to each leaseholder over a few months, which must contain certain information and provide them the opportunity to be part of the process, including the actual specification and choice of contractor.

The Problems

Service charges in property management can be time bombs just waiting to explode. Their detail is often missed, with everyone assuming things are ticking along okay, but then it all comes to roost later on when the accounts are reconciled.

Get a clear understanding early on. Sift through specific details, such as the latest budget, the last few years' accounts of actual costs, and if there are any future plans for large expenditures. Remember that any potential repairs in the future may hit and increase the service charge, and for an item such as a shared flat roof, then there may come a time when it has to be replaced as a legitimate 'repair' rather than just patched up.

Check any sinking and reserve funds, if any exist, or are planned, and check that everyone has been fairly paying into it. Also try to speak directly with either the tenant or landlord and get the bottom line of what this all means, as you can often go around the houses with replies on paper through solicitors in a letting or sale or when you receive new service charge details.

If things are still not clear and not getting resolved, then check with others, maybe other tenants or previous landlords. Request specific details if needed, although there may be an administration charge for supplying this. Also check out how this all hangs together long term and whether short-term tenants of, say, a year should be involved in much longer-term costs at the property.

If all else fails, then see what mechanism you can use to formally query and bring in a third party to resolve. With residential property, there is the legislation as well as lease terms, and with businesses, there may be options in the lease, or you can check if the landlord or the agent is part of an accreditation scheme and should be following best practice.

As an example, I was involved in a residential estate where certain house plots paid under £100 per year towards the upkeep of the shared car parking areas. Two things emerged here, firstly that this is not a usual service charge through a lease but rather maintenance charges through restrictions in the land title, which do follow similar principles but are governed by land restrictions, not leases.

Secondly, there was no point in the proposed new plot owner spending further legal costs on endless questions, as the cost was so low anyway during the year that any savings would be outweighed by the legal costs of pursuing it. If they were paying £1000 per year for an apartment, then yes, it's worth digging deeper.

Landlord Focus: Remember that this is separate money to your own personal rent, or even insurance premium, to be held separately for the good of the actual occupiers at the property. If you have a managing agent appointed, then make sure they're regulated to manage these correctly in separate client bank accounts with clear procedures, and if you're doing it yourself, it's worth following similar principles.

Keep money clear, communicate realistic budgets, and close off and issue accounts quickly. Analyse what costs can be in the service charge carefully, and be ready to pay towards it yourself for any void units. Know what communication you need in what timescale, and see what longer-term works verge on improvements but which could wholly or partly still be through the service charge rather than your own pocket.

Investor Focus: Although not a direct liability, it can come back and bite you. Check that accounts are in order and that the current level is realistic and actually payable by tenants. Also see what long-term costs can be in the service charge to be paid by tenants and not the landlord; often, long-term refurbishment or even redevelopment work can pass some of the charges legitimately in the service charge, with the rest being covered by the owner direct unless there are void and unrecoverable parts, in which case you'll need to pick up that service charge part anyway. Be careful, though, not to inflate the service charge as this can deter new tenants and have an eventual negative effect on market rents and values.

Tenant Focus: Make sure you get to really understand what is happening here and that things are being done correctly. Half the battle is understanding what is going on, which, unfortunately, can mean that you are paying towards things that you may not realise you should and which may mean big bucks being due in the future. Typical examples include replacement machinery like heating and lifts and both internal and external decorations. Also, try to agree on a cap of the service charge right at the lease drafting stage so you know for certain the maximum you'll ever be charged.

24. Insurance

Key Points: Incorrect insurance cover can hit your pocket in many respects. Here's what you need to know:

- *The different policies*
- *Residential property*
- *The right premiums*
- *The hidden excess & VAT*
- *The correct compliance*
- *The successful claims*

The Different Policies

Very crudely, there are two types of insurance cover. First is buildings insurance, which covers the main building structure and things that are logically fixed to it, although separate engineering & plant insurance cover can be needed for larger items like lifts, boilers, and ventilation equipment. The policy will focus on the location and type of building brick by brick and how much it would cost to literally rebuild the property, often called the Reinstatement Value. This is different to the actual market value of the property and looks at the literal cost for a builder to rebuild rather than what it would sell for in the market.

You can also have a loss-of-rent cover, which will help cover any missing rent from a tenant who would not be able to occupy the property during any rebuild works and, under their lease, legitimately not need to pay rent or other costs like a service charge.

Top Tip: These Reinstatement Values need an accurate revaluation by a building surveyor or someone else who is qualified to do so, including how they may need to be split for different areas of a larger property. They then need reviewing every few years and can have standard uplifts on them in the meantime. Not only check any new policy but any existing or old figures and how accurate or dated they really are.

Secondly, there are insurance policies for what happens regarding the occupation of the building. So there's contents insurance, including any fixtures to the building, and loss-of-trade and BI (Business Interruption) cover as well.

There's also employers liability insurance, which can be for owners and managers as much as occupiers, with additional fidelity and employers protection insurance as well and public liability (or property owners liability) insurance to cover liability from the property itself (like falling masonry) if a third party is injured. Property managers also need to look at their own professional indemnity insurance in case they are sued by clients, landlords, tenants, or third parties for professional negligence, plus directors & officers cover is available for these roles that people have in management companies for example.

As an example of how these two types of insurance inter relate, imagine a house where someone breaks in by damaging the glass and frame in a window, and then they steal various kinds of expensive electronic items like a TV and laptop. These all need to be paid for through an insurance claim, and although the windows and glass may strictly be the responsibility of the tenant under a long lease they have at the property, they are logically part of the main building fabric, and the building insurance will cover a claim for that element. But the actual loss of electronic goods and the damage to the curtains and rails behind the window, which is classed as part of the tenant's fixtures, will need to be separately claimed for through the tenant's own contents insurance.

Residential Property

For short-term lets on ASTs, for example, the landlord will remain the party who pays the premium for the building insurance policy and is ultimately responsible for any issues with the cover. With long leasehold interests though, where the leaseholder pays directly or more often through the service charge, even though their immediate landlord may arrange this, there is legislation to protect them and ensure owners and managers procure things correctly, mainly through the Landlord & Tenant Act 1985 and Commonhold & Leasehold Reform Act 2002.

Leaseholders can ask a relevant Tribunal to nominate an alternative insurer if the landlord's cover is unsatisfactory or premiums are too high and can serve notices requesting a written summary of insurance cover within 21 days and request that the landlord send copies of the policy documents. The landlord can't charge for this (other than a reasonable charge for copying), although a long lease may allow separate charges. Leaseholders can also go directly to an insurer with written notification of a possible claim.

The Right Premiums

This is the annual amount paid to the insurance company for this cover, and although a lot of mainstream residential policies will look at monthly direct debit payments, ones for larger and business polices will often need this paid up front or within an agreed grace period of, say, 30 days after cover starts.

Obviously, shop around for the best policy, although one word of warning: for larger and more complicated properties and scenarios, you may need to deal with specialist insurance companies and need the help of a middle-man insurance broker to help shop around and correctly specify as well as help with any issues regarding compliance and any claims you need in the future.

Top Tip: Ask what any broker is receiving on commission. This is often all included with the total premium you pay them or the insurance company and can be over 50% of the cost. They should declare this anyway, and any further middle-men, like managing agents, should clarify if they also get a slice and 'kick-back' from the insurers and that they are correctly regulated to deal with insurance matters.

Finally, see who the end person is who needs to pay this insurance, maybe the tenant through the lease or the service charge. The premium may then be split between them, and often the owner still needs to pays the insurance company or broker directly but then does a separate recharge invoice for the tenant or other party.

The Hidden Excess and VAT

On a successful claim, there may be an excess payment to pay, which the insurers may deduct from the final pay-out. Check who needs to cover this, maybe the tenant or the service charge, as it can suddenly be noted as an under pay-out afterwards.

Also, check the VAT status because if you can't claim it back but you need to incur it on contractors carrying out repairs, this should be included in the pay-out.

The Correct Compliance

The insurers may give you terms and conditions as well as actions to take within certain timescales of days or months, for example if the property is vacant then insisting on regular inspections, turning utility supplies off, and sealing any post boxes.

It's important that these are checked, understood, and clarified with the insurers over what they mean. Also, it's critical to have clear, written backup of these being completed and monitored as this could cause you problems with insurers paying out later on. A landlord then needs to check if any occupier tenant needs to implement some of these things, as stated in their lease.

Top Tip: Also watch out for whose name the insurance policy is in and what interests are noted on it as this can affect how others are also involved. Normally it is just the landlord/owner's name, but co-insured or composite insured are becoming more popular (sometimes known as a lenders or mortgagee protection clause), where your mortgage lender or other interests, like a freeholder, are joint-insured, often dictated by a loan or long lease agreement. They will need to also be notified and involved with any claims, including deciding whether a pay-out or actual re-build is warranted, and agree to any change of insurers. This is where a good insurance broker is needed to clearly explain things.

The Successful Claims

If you do need to make a claim, often you need several quotes for the repair works, and you need to go through the insurer's own procedures and application form. Think firstly about whether, in fact, it's worthwhile, even progressing with a claim particularly with smaller ones, after taking into account any excess payments to deduct or notes on the policy, which will cause future premium increases.

Landlord Focus: You must get this right for the building's cover and be clear that it covers everything and that everyone does what they should do to validate it. Break down the figures to check any commissions and small-print terms and conditions.

Investor Focus: Make sure this is covered okay to protect your investment, and be clear on who needs to pay the bill in terms of the premium and extras as this will affect your end valuation, including the ability to recharge in leases.

Tenant Focus: As well as looking at your own contents and business insurance, clarify how this links with the buildings insurance and also if you're paying the bill for the buildings insurance anyway through your lease.

25. Fees & Charges

Key Points: *There can be extra charges raised that you don't expect, so here's what you need to look out for:*

- *Application costs*
- *Landlord processing costs*
- *Problem costs*
- *Other costs*

Application Costs

When a tenant first takes a property, there can be the initial cost of vetting them and completing the lease and paperwork. This can sometimes be due even at the point of application with no guarantee of even being accepted at the property, particularly through the landlord's letting agents, so make sure you're focused on seeing things through.

Landlord Processing Costs

If a landlord has to do something to assist the tenant in some action, then they can often request a reasonable charge for this according to the lease; for example, if the landlord needs to grant formal permission to a subtenant or alterations at the property.

This is often stated in the lease, although not the actual amounts due, which will need clarifying. These can escalate to steamy heights of thousands, not just hundreds of pounds once the landlord has to involve other advisors such as building surveyors or solicitors. From a tenant's perspective, it can feel like the landlord has you over a barrel as they may seem too much, but the hassle and time delay in arguing can outweigh the benefit of just getting agreed. Try to liaise with and agree upon a fair solution for everyone.

Top Tip: This is more landlord focused when talking about costs being charged, but as a tenant, look at ways to agree any of your own costs being covered, either by open discussion with the landlord or agreeing in a side letter or even the lease draft. Maybe you are involved in doing 'extras' at the property, like checking any shared areas of the property or helping coordinate the landlord's contractors on site. Also, if you ever had difficulty in chasing issues with the landlord, then look at including these as well.

Problem Costs

These are costs involved in sorting out problems, two popular examples being chasing arrears and sorting out repairs and dilapidations at the end of the lease. Again, check the lease, making sure everything is included, and make sure they don't soon escalate and become out of context to the original issue.

Other Costs

There will be other people involved as well, whether surveyors, solicitors, or estate and letting agents. Know what you may get caught with paying towards, what you have to cover, and what you can recharge to someone else. You will probably be the one who has to first pay these if you instruct them, and then separately recharge this to someone else rather than asking the third party to invoice the end-payer directly, although in reality, this may be worth trying to achieve.

For residential long leasehold property, any demand for administration charges must be accompanied by a summary of leaseholder rights and obligations regarding these proposed costs.

Top Tip: Sometimes these third-party costs may be recoverable through the service charge rather than tenants directly, although these are eventually therefore covered by tenants (and possibly landlord) anyway.

Landlord Focus: This is often an opportunity to get a lot of your costs covered, so it's worth seeing what is in existing leases or adding into new ones. Get these clarified and agreed with the tenant, including any recharges, as it can soon become costly and timely to sort out afterwards even though in theory they may all be due for payment by the tenant.

Investor Focus: Some of your own costs may also be recoverable from others, for example, insurance revaluations and general condition surveys. Also watch out for any aborted sale or letting costs being covered and budgeted for.

Tenant Focus: Be aware of costs that your landlord can often charge back to you as well as looking at opportunities to agree your own costs being covered by them as well. Always try and sensibly agree them rather than taking these at face value.

26. Rates & Council Tax

Key Points: *This is a huge property cost so easily missed, where in actual fact there are a few options available to reduce these:*

- *Get the right basis and figures*
- *Check exemptions and reliefs*
- *Private rent licences*

Get the Right Basis and Figures

With residential property, you'll pay council tax; with business properties, you'll pay business rates. Both go to your local authority, but the parameters are determined by larger government bodies. It's a form of tax designed for the user of a property to pay to reflect all the wider services by the local authority for the good of the local community.

For business premises in some areas, particularly city centres, there can also be an additional BID charge (Business Improvement District), where the idea is that local businesses chip in to a BID entity, which only uses that extra money for things in that particular area, maybe extra street cleaning or plant pots to improve the local vicinity.

Make sure these bills are correct, that the effective dates are right, and that whatever rateable value and multiplier and transitional effect or banding they have applied is correct. Try calling the local authority and chatting through, asking them to explain in plain English, or check out specialist rates advisors who can help advise.

In some cases, particularly with business properties, you can agree for the whole property to be removed from rates charges if, say, it is stripped and unusable space, or you can request reductions if there are unforeseen local circumstances around your area that are out of your control and seriously affecting your business, such as road works.

For residential property, there are council tax charges with similar principles and a set valuation band for your type and size of property applied against a charge rate set by your local authority. There are then specific adjustments for what individuals actually reside there, for example, percentage reduction for just a single adult and then particular groups of people, such as those with disabilities or students. You also need to check how any different use may affect this, such as a second home, or in a different area, such as holiday lets, and which may be worth changing to the business-rates regime.

Check Exemptions and Reliefs

Some properties and uses within property are completely exempt from needing to pay any rates or council tax, such as listed buildings or places of worship. Make sure these are agreed upon, particularly if there has been any material change in the building and circumstances.

In addition, there are scenarios where you can at least get temporary relief from having to pay anything in your situation at this particular point in time, even though the property is still classed as chargeable under normal circumstances. A good example is when the property is physically unoccupied for a period of time and no one is there to benefit from local services. This can often be after someone has left, and both residential and commercial property types have different periods of time, from a few weeks to a few months.

These void exemption periods have dramatically reduced over the years and can cause serious issues to the property owner when they are back to having to pay full rates even though no one is in the property and there is no rental income or sale proceeds. Certain schemes have therefore emerged over the last few years to try to combat this, particularly with commercial property when you tend to deal with bigger numbers, which includes moving in and out of a property to keep triggering the initial exception period or allowing a temporary occupation to an entity like a registered charity, which may be able to agree to a reduction in rates by at least 80%.

Top Tip: When a tenant leaves and a new tenant occupies, make sure you're clear about when their physical occupation date is and therefore trigger for rates or council tax, which will tend to look at physical occupation as the judge, not any lease dates. So if the lease ends on 31 December but the tenant actually leaves by 30 November, inform the local authority to only charge them to then and the landlord from 1 December. This helps the tenant but eats into any initial exception for the landlord, although one way to get around this is to add clauses in the lease to say if this is permitted.

Private Rent Licences

This is actually nothing to do with the rates or the council tax system, but because it is still through the local authority and can incur a charge, it can be mistaken to fall into the same category. For private rented houses, often in the London area, the local authority can request a licence to be applied for and issued to permit a separate letting of the property, not only on the basis of HMOs and multiple users but as a single family household. Check out what your local authority has in place on this.

Landlord Focus: Although you won't tend to get involved with this as it is the tenant who's obliged to pay these liabilities directly, the problems come when the property is empty. It is worth looking into beforehand and working with the tenant to try to process any changes. However, be aware as well that because these are such substantial costs that a tenant has, it can have a knock-on effect to what they pay as rent and their financial sustainability.

Investor Focus: You have to not only be careful of being hit with any direct charges but even when the tenant pays directly, then any excessive rates can indirectly affect the rental and open market value for the property. As above, plan for any void periods and rates-mitigation opportunities, and be aware that sometimes it's worthwhile to keep an old tenant and lease on simply so they maintain the rates/tax liability.

Tenant Focus: Carefully check what the charges are, and request proposed charges from the local authority or previous tenants or landlords. Look at ways to reduce, and check how you may need to involve the landlord in this process.

27. Tax

Key Points: *It's inevitable to end up paying tax somewhere; therefore, here are some of the issues to consider in order to mitigate this liability:*

* *VAT*
* *Taxes within accounts*
* *Stamp Duty Land Tax*
* *Non-resident landlord*

VAT

The most important distinction to make here is between the actual property and people, something most people won't comprehend and therefore ends up causing all kinds of problems. Think of the property as an 'asset', something that is sellable like any other commodity that may or may not attract a VAT charge on it. Sometimes they do, sometime they don't; and sometimes they are automatically not, but you can elect to make them so in order to bring things into the VAT world and claim back VAT charges on things you've spent at the property.

Then look at whether individual parties are VAT elected or not, which will depend upon their own circumstances, their nature, and the volume of turnover. So if the property is in the VAT world, then a landlord or tenant who is VAT registered, either compulsory or by choice, can deal with this charge okay in their VAT returns and claim back. But if not, then any VAT charge cannot be processed and therefore becomes like another 20% on the charge. This is critical in new lettings of property with smaller business tenants who cannot absorb this VAT. So a £5,000 per year rent to them is basically a £6,000 expenditure.

Taxes Within Accounts

In very crude terms, you tend to get taxed on your income side, and then taxed on your capital and investment side. Further details are in the realm of accountancy and will look carefully at whether people are individuals or in vehicles such as partnerships and companies.

The important thing to remember is that by receiving an income from property, like rent, you may get charged tax. On the occupation side, if you have to pay these kinds of running costs, then they can be helpful deductions to your tax liability. On the capital side, for a landlord or investor, see how this property is to be held in the accounts, what taxes are incurred when things are sold or bought, and how they are treated in things like balance sheets.

Top Tip: Remember to include all the figures and types of income and expenditure from a tax and accounting perspective, even if it's paid indirectly. So if you have a flat investment, you may be paying utilities like water and maybe even electricity for your own flat, within the service charge not just the communal areas, which you may need to quantify.

Top Tip: Check with an accountant about things like Capital Allowances, which can be applicable for the element of a property purchase towards the fixed plant or machinery there rather than the literal property. You'll also need to consider the previous owner's claim for such allowances and how it may now affect yours.

Top Tip: another more recent change to carefully check that will affect private residential buy-to-let landlords in particular is the reduction in tax relief on their mortgage interest and only a basic rate of tax being able to be claimed.

Stamp Duty Land Tax

Stamp Duty Land Tax is a tax incurred when a property interest is sold or a notable lease interest completes for a certain length of lease and rent but also when the lease may change or be extended later on. The amount is based upon the value of the transaction, with a certain minimum level first needed and then possible reliefs, and it affects both residential and commercial property.

This can be a real surprise for both owners of new property but also occupiers taking new and large lease interests, therefore, it is important to determine at the outset if this is going to be liable and, to see if there will be any recalculations in the future, particularly with rent reviews in leases. Then see if there are any alternative ways to structure or negotiate a transaction to mitigate these costs, for example, the sale of a company holding a property interest rather than just the property interest itself.

Non-Resident Landlord

For those landlords that are based abroad but involved with UK property and monies, there needs to be a process of registering with HMRC as non-resident landlords for tax purposes, and this will determine if tax needs to be deducted and paid here in the UK.

Landlord Focus: You'll need accountancy advice on these issues, although once the principles are correctly established, you may be able to do a lot yourself in terms of bookkeeping and completing and returning your tax return online. Include advice on how to mitigate these in general, maybe in the way you hold the property, allowable expenses, and reduce other taxes like VAT and rates.

Investor Focus: This is critical to get the most out of your property investment, particularly the way in which the property is legally held and how each property interest is noted in your accounts. You'll also need to understand what the real-life cash profit is that you can withdraw from the investment, not just profit and assets held on paper.

Tenant Focus: This will still apply to you, particularly the way in which you treat all these expenses of property occupation. Look at all costs as well, not just the basic rent, and how these need to be accounted for.

28. Valuations & Mortgages

Key Points: *What a building is worth and arranging mortgages on it is often the bottom-line aim of property ownership, so here are some aspects to consider:*

- *Types of valuations*
- *Mortgage principles*
- *Letting v. buying*

Types of Valuations

There are four main ways to approach a property valuation, and although the technicalities of them are not necessarily needed to be understood as it's the final value that matters, it's helpful to know what angle a valuer will come from, what information they will require, and what factors of your property management will affect the figures.

Firstly, there is the comparable method. This looks at say what a similar house goes for down the road and tweaks the price or rent by any differences, such as being in better condition or having no parking. Secondly, there is a way of looking at what income is derived from the property, mainly rent, and applying a suitable yield and other kinds of adjustments to end up with an end value. Thirdly, there is a way of looking more at the constriction-cost side deducted from potential income or sale values less profit to then arrive at land values, particularly suitable for redevelopments and land where you look at the land and construction costs. Fourthly, for very unique properties that depend more on the unique use they have, you look more at the profits from that particular business, so maybe restaurants and pubs.

Top Tip: This can also apply to tenants, particularly long-leasehold ones, where there is value in having that interest over a long period of time and paying only a ground-rent, not market rent. This is a specialised area and can involve 'marriage value' with long leasehold residential property and the potential extra value of also purchasing the freehold title.

Mortgage Principles

This is obviously a specialised financial area, suffice to say that it's worth thinking about the purpose of your property interest and requirements to make sure your funding arrangements are correct. Look at whether it's an interest-only or full payment mortgage, and check if the interest and capital parts of your monthly payments will have an effect on your accounts. Can there be any payment 'holidays' if times get tough, and what requirements will the mortgage company have on running the property and dealing with the lease and tenants day to day?

Also, think about any re-mortgaging opportunities in the future, or when you sell the property, and the ability to gear-up and leverage any equity in your property to start developing a property portfolio. (There are lots of property investment books already available along these lines.)

Letting v. Buying

The British love the idea of owning things; our home is our castle and our business premises our territory. As well as this feel-good factor and freedom to use your own space, you've got a nice investment there with your money paying it off rather than wasted rent.

Bear in mind, though, that the general market reality of higher property prices, increased deposit requirements, rising demand for homes in particular, and reduced supply of property means reality can be a little different. Other European countries make do with a more letting culture, and this is increasingly becoming the case in the UK with specialist markets like the PRS (Private Rented Sector) evolving with property investors.

So have a reality check, but think outside of the box to see how this can change over time. Maybe go smaller and cheaper now and save a deposit. Can you involve family members with the mortgage or guarantor, and can you hold business property in other investor and pension vehicles? Can you even look at renting a property with an option-to-buy later on or agree on a reduced rent if the landlord will allow you to decorate and fit out more to your tastes if you're going to be there longer term?

Top Tip: Go one step further, and look at crazy ideas of living cheaper, whether caravans, converting larger properties into smaller units, or making use of outbuildings and land.

Landlord Focus: This will, of course, relate directly to you, so make sure the figures stack up with how you own and finance the property, with rental income covering it, and being prepared for any one-off costs, and developing a longer-term strategy.

Investor Focus: This will be what it's all about, so make sure you have a full exit strategy and prepare to build and stretch the portfolio as well as being ready financially for any other asset-management opportunities.

Tenant Focus: Although less applicable, start looking at ways to eventually own your own property as well. For longer-term leases, see what value you already have there and what options, such as part subletting or lodgers, may have on the figures.

29. Accounts

Key Points: Getting your accounts on top of is one of the most critical aspects of property management, and although it can take a while for issues to emerge, when they do, it can be costly. Here are some of the main aspects to consider:

- *Different types of money and bank accounts*
- *Regulation and systems*
- *Cash and bank reconciliations*
- *Invoices and receipts*
- *Arrears*
- *Presenting accounts*

Different Types of Money and Bank Accounts

There are four main 'pots' of money involved with property management, the first being the obvious one of rent and any sales proceeds. These ultimately belong to the property owner/investor/landlord, which they may collect directly into their bank or through appointed solicitors or managing agents.

The second is service charges as referred to earlier, and the third is insurance premiums, which can be part of the service charge or a separate recharge to tenants but which is kept aside to pay the insurers. The fourth is any odd bits and bobs to charge, maybe fees to the landlord or tenant, or dealing with other charges.

You need to be clear about these monies and keep them as separate a possible, particularly the first rent and sales proceeds, which belong directly to the owner, who may need to receive this directly and quickly in order to then pay the mortgage.

Regulation and Systems

If you involve third parties like a managing agent, solicitor, estate or letting agent, or other professionals, then they should be regulated. Some are by law, for example, those under the Financial Services Authority like mortgage brokers, and of course solicitors. Others should be involved in a regulatory scheme as good practice; for example, you could employ anyone to be your managing agent, whereas a Chartered Surveying firm will be regulated by the RICS or they could be a member of say the Institute of Residential Property Management (IRPM).

In short, these regulations will bring safeguards. Money needs to be kept in separate bank accounts that only authorised people can transfer in and out, and there will be insurance cover in case things do go wrong.

There should also be a nicely working property accounts 'department' that not only easily accounts for all these monies but can easily send out understandable reports and maybe even have online access for clients to access directly.

Cash and Bank Reconciliations

These are critical but are often missed by anyone not naturally an accountant. Basically, every single transaction that is made within property management, every penny received, and every one spent within a period of a month, for example, must match up with the bank transactions so that there is a clear trail of transactions that 'reconcile'. This sounds simple, but if this gets out of sync, then there can be big issues later on, even years ahead, particularly with old service charges to close down and trying to check whether such and such a repair was actually paid for by the landlord's rent money direct or the service charge pot and whether that was the correct way to do it.

Top Tip: If someone else is doing this, ask for proof. If you liaise with a non-accounting property manager, they may not realise what goes on behind the scenes with the accounts. Even ask your own accountant and bookkeeper to check these, and make sure they match up and are reported correctly to match your own accounts, tax, and VAT purposes.

Invoices and Receipts

As well as bank statements, you will still need documentation in the form of invoices and receipts to prove any monies like rent that you have received and monies you have spent, say, from a supplier like the electricity company. This will back up the books nicely and save you endless hassle later on.

Top Tip: The payment of supplier invoices like the electricity bills and gardener can become a role in itself known as Accounts Payable. With smaller scenarios, this just becomes part of the other accounting tasks, but as it gets more complicated, particularly with using different pots of cash and service charges, it may be worth outsourcing just this element.

Two words of caution though here. Firstly, make use of the Internet, but make sure it doesn't become a burden. Utility suppliers are a good example where they have online accounts for you to access nowadays, but this can be a real pain to get login details, whereas often you just want a simple invoice. Also, make use of digital versions of things, so you may not even need to see them literally on paper, just sent on email, or you can then store them on your computer until needed by your accountant.

Secondly, don't get too carried away with generating paperwork when you don't really need it. An example is when tenants will often want further remittances to confirm when an actual payment has been received, which can become another series of paperwork.

Top Tip: Knowing the cash situation as well as the situation on paper is critical and often missed. So you may, on paper, have a perfect service charge budget to pay everything, but if you have a few tenants not paying up or a large electricity bill suddenly going out, you may practically not have the cash in the bank yet, and therefore this may need funding by the owner until monies start coming back in.

Arrears

Arrears, otherwise known as Credit Control, is essential to keep on top of what's owed—when people owe you money, you need to chase them. Common ones are tenants for landlords, but you may have third parties like solicitors or estate agents that need to pay monies over to you.

In the ideal world, you shouldn't need to do this, but unfortunately you do. In the majority of situations, people either genuinely forget or there is an administration glitch somewhere, like they didn't receive your invoice, they don't know the bank details, or the name on the invoice is wrong. So work out some kind of procedure, which may be just a gentle phone call or email or, on the other extreme, a process with a managing agent to send reminder letters.

There will be those that still don't pay though, and you'll need to know what the next course of action is; it may involve threatening action or taking other options as detailed earlier.

Presenting Accounts

After all this works goes on behind the scenes, work out how it will all come together, including helpful reports that actually make sense to the layperson, who often just want to know the bottom-line figures, like how much money was collected and how much was spent. But also make sure there is enough detail here for, say, an accountant who then needs to do say your annual tax return or quarterly VAT return.

Also be aware of what accounts you may need to prepare for your property interest, whether a landlord or investor with a serious property business needing profit-and-loss and balance sheets or a tenant occupier where the property costs can be a genuine expenditure in your business accounts.

All existing UK accounting standards were actually replaced by a single standard in January 2015, and it's important to understand through an accountant just what the true money situation is on paper and the consequences of this. As investment properties are assets held for generating rental income or capital appreciation, check what changes occur in the profit-and-loss account as well as balance sheet, considering factors such as revaluations, lease incentives, deferred tax, construction contracts, and the end effects of values, tax liability, and bank covenants.

Landlord Focus: You must keep on top of this as it will be easy to miss if you're not wired up like an accountant, which can cause serious problems later on. On one side, make sure things are done correctly from an accountant's perspective, with your own individual or firm checking things and procedures. On the other, make sure you know how all this works out in reality and where invoices go, when payments come in, and how you know the bottom-line cash scenario.

Investor Focus: Your focus needs to be more on what you own now and how involved you'll be in the day-to-day money matters so you get the true picture and don't have any nasty surprises later on that will cost you, as the buck and bill will ultimately stop with you, the property owner and investor.

Tenant Focus: Understand what is going on, know what any charges are for, and make sure that money is kept safe. Where it's separate money like service charge and insurance, you'll have rights to know more about this, particularly with residential property.

30. Grants

Key Points: Check to see if there are any other areas of funding available for your property interest, for example:

- *Looking at all options*
- *Checking compliance*
- *Thinking of others*

Looking at All Options

The world of grants and funding is complicated and involves lots of completely different avenues. Put simply, it's going to be best to carry out your own research on the Internet, ask others, and check with local property professionals and local authorities. Think outside the box in terms of the property side and works of improvements, such as energy-efficiency measures, but also the situation with people generally and their ability to receive this kind of support.

Checking Compliance

Whatever you look into, check the small print. Check what you need to first comply and then what you need to do afterwards so it's not invalidated. If needed, search for a specialist in this area to advise, but still make sure they are in a position to do so themselves, and even check things like their own insurance being in place in case things go wrong.

As an example, years ago a property owner successfully secured funding for works on a listed building to convert to residential. They didn't realise, though, that they had to pay this all back if the property was sold so many years afterwards, so they were forced to retain and rent out, not ideal at the start of the recession, when prices started to then fall.

Thinking of Others

You may not be in a position yourself for grants and funding, but mention this to others, like your landlord or tenant or other advisors, if you think it is applicable. As well as the basic helping-others principle, it may indirectly benefit you anyway by additional value to the property or reducing running costs.

Landlord Focus: Check what can be available for you, although note that the benefits may often easily filter down to the tenant and not necessarily yourself straightaway, although with larger building-focused works, these will often pay off over time.

Investor Focus: As well as building matters, look at other issues, such as the location of the property and the benefits this brings and the way and mechanism that you are holding the property.

Tenant Focus: Look at what will help you directly, and don't get too carried away doing your landlord's job for them. Energy efficiency is an obvious one and may be worth you working with your landlord on measures like this.

THE PAPERWORK PERSPECTIVE

31. Leases and Agreements

Key Points: This may sound laborious, but leases or any other agreement should really be fully read throughout to really know what you've signed up to. Here are some of the main issues to be looking for:

- *Nature of the agreement*
- *Commercial property*
- *Residential property*
- *Heads of terms*
- *Demised areas*
- *Use of the property*
- *Improvements and reinstatement*
- *Alienation*

Nature of the Agreement

The document that clarifies how someone uses another person's property is often referred to as a 'lease', although it's important to realise the legal implications of this and situations where, in fact, it is another form of agreement. A lease confers definite rights in writing, should be correctly signed, and provides 'exclusive possession' to a tenant from a landlord, and clarifies basic parameters like a definite term and rent.

Other agreements, like a licence, which is not as 'exclusive' as a lease, can actually turn into a lease with all the rights and responsibilities that go with it. There are also others, such as a Tenancy at Will or Periodic Tenancy, and leases can also be completed to only take effect in the future (Reversionary leases), or completed now for a time in the future when the property or land is suitable for use (a Pre-let lease).

Although there is no standard lease, you can use good templates from property authorities like the Law Society and RICS, and since 2006, all longer leases needing registration at the Land Registry need set, prescribed clauses at the beginning with information like the date of lease and term, existing land registration title numbers, the parties, a description of the property, the premium paid, restrictive covenants and easements, and other information and statutory rights involved.

There are also sales contracts to be aware of, with any standard conditions or ones specifically agreed for that transaction, plus separate agreements to purchase or transact an interest in land depending upon circumstances like securing planning permission and involving other parties, such as funders, insurers, contractors, and developers.

To get your head around this, first check any existing agreements yourself. Make sure you receive copies, even if it means asking your landlord or tenant for ones if you don't have copies in your records. Secondly, make sure they're correct, that they're signed properly, and that there are additional documents with it as necessary, for example, Licence of Alterations or regarding lease extensions. Thirdly, get this clarified by someone who knows the legal implications, whether a solicitor or other advisor, to help determine what this means in reality, both during and after the agreement formally ends.

Commercial Property

Most commercial property will be occupied through leases, which tend to give control and obligations for the property to the tenant. So this often includes the main structure and services, or obligations to pay towards it in a multi-let property, with generally less service-charge legislation control than residential.

You can also come across licences for short-term temporary occupation or other forms of leases, such as Tenancies at Will and Periodic Tenancies, although the majority are through business property leases that are available generically from the Law Society or through solicitors and then modified, and with certain legislation implying certain rights and obligations, particularly under the Landlord & Tenant Act 1954.

In locations with more complicated land and lease ownerships, the actual ownership of a business property may need to be through, say, a 999-year lease rather than freehold, for example, in out-of-town small office parks.

Residential Property

Leases for residential property fall into two types. The first one includes long leases, which are aimed to provide long-term ownership rights for buildings where the actual freehold can't be held by multiple people, for example, a block of flats that need separate flat ownership documents as opposed to a detached house that could be held as one freehold.

There is a host of legislation shaping such long leases and implying rights on both the owner 'tenant' and the main ultimate freeholder or management company or superior lease-holder landlord to help provide greater protection and security for people's homes and residences.

The second type is short-term lets and occupation, whether a residential owner holds the property freehold or through their own long lease ownership as above and they want a short-term tenant there for perhaps six months or a few years. The most popular short-term agreement is an Assured Shorthold Tenancy agreement (AST) for self-contained residential units, which allows a landlord to charge whatever rent can be agreed upon and obtain possession without justification provided the fixed term has expired or there has been a legitimate break and the tenant has been there for at least six months.

However, there are others, such a AST for a room only and Excluded Tenancy (Lodger) Agreement, a Owner-Occupier Tenancy Agreement, a Company Let Agreement where you're dealing with a corporate tenant name rather than an individual, and a Non Assured Tenancy Agreement.

There was a change in the nature of short-term residential tenancies in 1989 so that one's started prior to this are Regulated Tenancies and ones after are Assured Tenancies, of which an Assured Shorthold Tenancy is one form.

Not all of these have 'assured shorthold tenancy' rights like the popular AST, but where they do this provides rights under the Housing Act 1988 and an obligation to protect deposits under a government-approved scheme. You also deal with obtaining possession and collecting arrears through certain procedures with a court order, and automatically continues on after the fixed term unless certain steps are taken.

Top Tip: Make sure any occupation is correctly documented, as a legal 'tenancy' can still exist without a written agreement if under three years, and still giving the tenant Housing Act protection. A tenant is entitled to a written agreement within 28 days of the start from a landlord or their agent.

Top Tip: With residential property, there may also be other forms of co-ownership within the social housing sector, such as the statutory Right to Buy for tenants and Shared Ownership leases. Also, the Commonhold & Leasehold Reform Act 2002 introduced a new form of ownership of communal areas within shared residential developments known as commonhold as detailed earlier.

Heads of Terms

These are basically a summary of the main points agreed for any new letting or sale, such as rent or sale price, length of lease, and the parties involved. They're more popular with business property, and it's handy to include as much information in these as possible in order to assist solicitors as they draft actual agreements, for example, any rights allowed, full contact details of the parties, and how you're dealing with smaller issues like utilities and service charges.

Although they are not binding formal agreements, they could be used to imply things later on, so make sure these are 'subject to contract' and just the starting point of the legal documentation.

Demised Areas

This is one of the most overlooked areas of a lease, just what the area of a building is that is being given to an occupier. Yes, it should be simple, like a specific house address or a ground floor shop on a parade, but add as much detail as possible regarding the exact address, including the post code and full postal address, other plot numbers with new developments, and details such as any external areas and car parking being included. Also, literally what elements of the building are included, such as the internal finishes only of the walls and ceiling and floor and not the main structure, and whether it includes details such as windows and doorframes.

Top Tip: Also detail services, or 'conduits', such as water/gas/electricity and literally what is included within a 'demise'. Leases often say something like those exclusively serving, which will include any cables/pipes outside your property from a communal point or meter in the road or with the next-door neighbour for example, even if they fall outside your main area.

Use of the Property

Clarify this as far as possible as either a general description or, as in the case of business property, they can refer to specific types of business uses according to the planning 'Use Classes' under The Town & Country Planning (Use Classes) Order 1987.

Remember that on one hand you may want this restricted so that it controls who can use the property and how they use it as well as control the number of other competitive occupiers. However, this can cause restrictions in use later on and filter down to reduce valuations and rents. You can maybe get around this by the use being allowed to change in the future subject to the landlord's approval, although be careful as the landlord is not restricted under general legislation to be 'reasonable' in their decision unless it specifically says so in the lease.

In addition to the main user clause in any lease or contract, there can be other restrictions in the use of the property, which tends to relate more to the practical issues with property management, for example, no pets being allowed if it is a residential property, no dangerous chemicals stored, or even restricted opening hours.

As an example, if you have a flat above a shop in a parade, you may want to place restrictions in the lease to a new shop occupier so they don't cause a nuisance to the residential flats and the rest of the traders on the parade. Also, if the landlord owns the rest of the shops on the parade, then also check what all the other leases say. So maybe there is already a betting shop, which states that the landlord cannot allow another betting shop in another unit, therefore this shop may be let out to a convenience store instead; however, this tenant may want to make sure it is clarified that they can have early morning deliveries of bread and milk at 6 a.m. every morning without complaints from the residential tenants above.

Improvements and Reinstatement

This ends up being a big area of leases, which tends to come to light at the end of the agreement and needs thinking about in two stages.

Firstly, document correctly what additional works, improvements, and alterations the occupier is carrying out. This not only clarifies the consent of the landlord but helps resolve with other authorities, such as planning permission and building control consent.

In terms of then paying the cost of these works, often the tenant is paying for these, although check whether the landlord has agreed to pay towards or even offer a rent free at the start of the lease, and if meant to be reflected in any reviewed rent later on. This can be a double whammy for a tenant in that they not only have to pay for the works at the start but possibly increased rent from their own works afterwards. There are also procedures to go through so that a landlord can't refuse any sensible changes and so that the tenant is compensated for these improvements at the end of the lease, for example, through the Landlord & Tenant Act 1927 for business property leases.

Secondly, it needs to be clarified how the tenant leaves the building when they leave. This is often referred to as 'reinstatement' or 'yielding up', and it clarifies what the tenant must remove and take back out as well as the condition and any resultant repairs that must be carried out. Often this may be down to the landlord to decide what they want to keep, and the decision can affect what the tenant is then liable for in terms of what they need to leave in situ and in good condition. Items may be originally the tenant's but end up belonging to the landlord as part of the main building afterwards. (This can get complicated with talk of fixtures, fittings, and chattels.)

Top Tip: In any lease, as well as looking at what is left and what goes and who determines this, also make sure the procedure and timescale for doing this is clarified. So if the landlord does need to make a decision, then within, say, the last three months of the lease; otherwise, everyone assumes they are removed or remain.

Alienation

This is all about a tenant wanting to transfer a lease over to someone else and therefore being 'alienated' from it.

The two popular forms are subletting, where the tenant still has the main lease and control and responsibilities, or assignment, where the whole lease transfers over to another name. Even if they do assign over, the original tenant can still be on the hook afterwards automatically or by request which is helpful when a new tenant is perceived to not be as good a bet for the landlord. You then need to consider any other parts of the lease, like guarantors or lenders being party to these changes.

There are two other points to remember as well. Firstly, you can have agreements in joint names, although these two or more people are treated as one entity in legal terms, so if one is removed, then, in fact, the whole agreement can end. Secondly, be careful when you look at less permanent arrangements, including maybe just subletting part of your property or having lodgers. This whole area of 'alienation' is often clarified in the lease, so check that you're not in breach by a more informal temporary arrangement, and remember, it's often best to liaise directly with the landlord or tenant to see if this can be clarified or even agreed with additional documentation.

Landlord Focus: You not only need to get this right with your current tenant in mind but also consider any other leases you have with other tenants in the same or nearby buildings to make sure there are no clashes. Also, sift through any leases you inherit, and be careful of the implications of any changes you agree to ad hoc with a tenant as they can invalidate the lease or rights of pursuing the guarantors in the lease.

Investor Focus: Looking through any existing leases or new ones is essential to not only see how this may affect the end-value of the property but also to see if there are any potential pitfalls to be aware of or restrictions towards any future plans of the property to make changes and maybe even redevelopment.

Tenant Focus: Be careful what you sign up to and that any side agreements are correctly completed so that they carry weight. There is a lot of legislation helping tenants; however, leases can tend to be very detailed in the landlord's favour as well.

32. Ending Leases and Agreements

Key Points: *Knowing how to deal with leases ending is critical, both at their natural end-date and during the term. Here are the angles you need to be aware of:*

- *Natural lease ends and renewals*
- *Commercial property*
- *Residential property*
- *Surrender*
- *Forfeiture*
- *Break options*

Natural Lease Ends and Renewals

This is where the end date in the lease arrives and therefore the original 'term' in the lease stops. Logically, you may assume that's it and that the tenant can leave or the landlord can take the area back, although in reality, there is a host of legislation to protect leases and enable them to actually continue in effect beyond these dates whilst procedures are gone through by the landlord and tenant to truly end them later.

The logic is to protect the parties from the other side's behaviour, particularly for tenants so that landlords can't act ruthlessly and suddenly throw tenants out at the end of the lease. For residential property, this is understandable, so leases will continue and protect people's homes until the right time, but the same applies for business leases as well in a different form.

This is an area that you'll need specialist advice on. Do your own research, but if you're in a potentially awkward position, then get advice to not only confirm that you have the right angle in mind but that you correctly implement it. The timing of notices and events will be critical as well as the form of actual notice to the other party, some of which needs to happen still within the main lease length to prepare parties for the end.

There are also three money angles to be aware of: firstly, how the current rent being paid matches the market rent. If it is under, then a landlord will be more incentivised to swiftly renew the lease to a higher level or end the lease and re-let, whereas a tenant may want to deliberately stretch things out to benefit from this current rent. There can be things like interim rent, though, through the correct procedures in order to help make sensible adjustments to these gaps.

Secondly, consider if any compensation is due, typically from a landlord to the tenant. So there may be a good, valid reason for a landlord needing the building back, maybe to actually use themselves, but there may be circumstances where they need to pay compensation to the tenant to reflect their disturbance.

Thirdly, verify the costs involved in this, including when you involve other advisors like solicitors or surveyors. You'll probably need this help, but make sure costs don't get carried away, and be clear on whether you pay this yourself or if they can be recharged to the other side, particularly if they're not playing fair.

Commercial Property

Commercial business property leases are primarily protected through a piece of legislation called the Landlord & Tenant Act 1954. This actually originated just after the second world war, when business premises were scarce because of bomb damage; therefore, legislation started to stop landlords deciding to end a business's occupation for a better deal, particularly where a specific location plays such an integral part in the business's goodwill, for example, with retail premises.

For business premises benefiting from this protection, a landlord needs to consider serving a Section 25 notice under this legislation with clear intentions to agree a renewal of the lease or to contest a renewal lease. Alternatively tenants needs a Section 26 notice to request a renewal or Section 27 after the natural lease expiry to end the lease and liabilities three months afterwards. Ideally, parties will agree to a solution between themselves, or either can then apply to court for their intervention and timescale in determining the outcome of a new lease or expiry and any interim rental level during this period.

Residential Property

With residential property, there is a host of legislation regarding how leases are ended or renewed, dependent upon circumstances, types of agreements, occupation, and purpose. For the popular short-term AST agreements, unless a new one is then agreed at the end, they will lapse into a statutory periodic tenancy, which will automatically continue on unless a tenant leaves by the end date or serves a notice to quit or the landlord serves a notice seeking possession.

If a tenant stays on even a few days after the completion of the AST term agreement, the tenancy will automatically become a periodic tenancy (unless the agreements says a contractual periodic tenancy), which means it extends for the same length of time as the rent was paid before, whether weekly, monthly, etc., and notice of one of these periods in writing needs to be sent to the landlord to then end it. In reality, with monthly rents, this works out at two months to give a clear whole one month period's notice.

Top Tip: From a landlord's perspective here, still wait until the existing tenant has actually left the property after any notice, to be on the safe side. If the tenant has the capability of serving you notice yet does not hand over the possession of the vacant area, you're allowed to charge double rent for this extra period under section 18 of the Landlord & Tenant Act 1737.

A landlord needs to serve a Section 21 or Section 8 notice to gain possession, deal with any arrears, stop the process of automatic renewals and then apply to court for a Possession Order and afterwards for the court bailiff to evict the tenant if needs be. This can be a complicated and lengthy process designed to protect tenants from landlords easily evicting them and causing harassment, although this means that tenants can use it to their advantage to complicate and extend the whole process.

Residential occupiers are protected from unlawful eviction or harassment from landlords through the Eviction Act 1977, along with other protection through the Housing Act 1988 and Civil Procedures Rules 1998, meaning landlords can't evict a residential occupier without a court order unless it's under an excluded tenancy or licence.

Top Tip: If a tenant is offered a new Assured or Assured Shorthold Tenancy by a landlord, but at a much higher and seemingly unreasonable rent, then there is the right to apply to a Tribunal for rent disputes to have this settled.

With longer leasehold property, there is a 'lease extension' right under the Leasehold Reform, Housing and Urban Development Act 1993 for leaseholders in blocks of flats to have another 90 years' lease extension from the end of their current term on the same terms as the existing lease so long as they have held the lease for at least two years and the landlord is not exempt. A sensible premium cost must be paid by the tenant based upon 'marriage value' plus landlord's costs as negotiated with the landlord or agreed through a Tribunal.

You can find online calculations or have a desktop valuation completed to get an idea of this renewal premium, although a full valuation is best to get it right. The important thing to remember is that this lease is only there to document an ownership of the residential area to mirror almost freehold ownership, with a low ground or peppercorn rent paid every year, so there is a cost for the tenant to have this contractual right extended.

Tactically, it's best to look at a formal Section 42 notice sent correctly to a landlord, and will become important when the remaining lease length is below 80 years and it becomes more difficult to secure a mortgage on the interest. It can still be served just before a sale and then assign the benefit of this notice and right to the new owner.

Surrender

This is nice and easy when both the landlord and tenant mutually agree to simply end the lease early. Even though they're both fine with it, there are two words of caution.

Firstly, make sure this is correctly documented so it's legally enforceable as sometimes it may require an official Deed. Secondly, make sure all the loose ends are clarified, for example, what condition the building will be left in, whether the landlord intends to still raise any balancing service charge payments in the future even though the lease has needed, or whether this is an all-inclusive deal, in which case a premium from one party to the other may wish to be agreed in order to reflect this.

Forfeiture

This is when the landlord can look to forfeit and end the lease because of the tenant not complying with the lease terms, with the main piece of legislation governing this being Section 146 of the Law of Property Act 1925. Court action and procedures are often needed, although more direct action can be taken with rent arrears in business properties and, literally, the locks suddenly changed on the property to end the lease if the lease permits this as long as the landlord behaves correctly so as not to waive this right.

Quite rightly, the tenant will have options of appeal and relief from this for up to six months afterwards. There is also greater protection with residential property at this stage, with Tribunals as well as courts being involved in determining cases. So even though forfeiture will terminate the lease and matters now, a tenant can come back and ask for it to be reinstated if they comply.

Break Options

If there is a break option in the lease, then it's a natural time for a party to formally end the lease. There will often be a clear notice procedure for this and possibly conditions for this being valid, for example, the condition of the property being left and any arrears being paid. These will need to be carefully looked at as parties can get tripped up on this detail with the worst-case scenario of still being left with a remaining lease they don't actually want because some detail was missed to validate the break.

For residential property, it's okay to have a tenant's or mutual landlord or tenant's break option in fixed term tenancies, but a landlord-only break is deemed unfair and unenforceable.

Top Tip: Inserting break options into leases can be a practical way to maintain long term occupation without the hassle and cost of having to keep renewing the same lease. So instead of, say, three-year leases being continually renewed, why not a nine-year lease with three-year break options, which has the same desired effect of only three-year chunks, but things keep ticking along if all is otherwise okay.

Landlord Focus: You'll need to be particularly careful how you deal with lease renewals as the focus will be on protecting the tenant, including the options and costs involved in this.

Investor Focus: Watch out for opportunities to release greater value in the property from lease changes and re-gearing leases and agreeing renewals early on, and not just leaving things until the end of the agreement.

Tenant Focus: The good news is that the law is on your side when it comes to renewing leases, although the bad news is that things can be more black and white if they are stated within the lease, particularly if there are specific ways you need to action a break option for example.

33. Repairs & Inventories

Key Points: *Dealing with property repairs and the issues surrendering them need careful consideration, so here are some of the main issues to note:*

- *Leases and the law*
- *Repairs*
- *Inventories*
- *Dilapidations*
- *Repairs notice*
- *Decorations*
- *Liabilities*

Leases and the Law

Firstly, look at any lease or sale agreement to see what it says about repairs. Sift through the whole agreement as there may be different clauses scattered around on different aspects, and check what indirect liabilities there may also be, for example, costs through a service charge that a landlord needs to carry out but the occupier ends up paying for.

Secondly, remember that there may be general legislation to clarify meanings in the lease or to provide specific duties to certain parties. In general, what is agreed in a new lease decides the outcome, in which case general legislation will clarify where the lease is silent.

With residential property, there is a whole raft of obligations for a landlord to repair the structure of the building, services, electrics, heating gas, etc., for short-term lets up to seven years long under legislation like the Landlord & Tenant Act 1985 as well as more general obligations under the Defective Premises Act 1972 and general principles of fitness for 'human habitation'. However, the landlord does need to be aware of these issues in reality, including within the demised residential area, hence the importance of regular inspections and tenants formally notifying them of any problems.

There are also external parties to consider, for example, local housing authorities under the Housing Act 2004, where they can take action such as improvement notices or demolition orders if there are houses and flats not meeting minimum conditions.

Top Tip: If you come across any land contamination and pollution issues, this can open a whole can of worms under the Environmental Protection Act 1990 in terms of identifying who ultimately is responsible, including the original polluter, and how this then needs resolving and clarifying.

Repairs

It is a fundamental obligation for people to keep the property in 'repair'. The actual wording of any repairing liability though can affect how far you go with repairs, with words like 'renew' or 'replace' often meaning what they say on the tin and not just a quick repair or 'bodge'.

You also have to be careful what areas of the property you're liable for, particularly within any lease arrangement but also purchase agreements and land titles. You may be involved in having to directly maintain or contribute towards a shared access driveway as per a land title restriction, or in a lease for a shared roof. However it may be directly outside your demise and therefore direct responsibility, although the landlord may be able to recharge you any repair costs through a service charge or on a one-off charge basis.

Inventories

This is where you take a record of the condition of the property at the start, often referred to as an inventory or schedule of condition. Before getting into the details of what they are, first check how they are referred to in the lease or other documents, an obvious point that is often missed. There needs to be a specific mention of this, for example, stating that the tenant has to keep the property in good repair but in no better condition than the schedule or inventory.

In terms of the actual inventory or schedule, it basically notes the condition of the building at one point in time, and you need to make sure it's not only accurate but has enough information in it as possible. This is particularly so with residential property, where it will need to be accurate in order to be valid later. So go around every room in the house, including storage areas never really used, lofts, etc., and even the outside areas and main structure. Take lots of photos—they can easily be on your mobile phone as you walk around—and include a mix of wider shots of a whole room but more detailed shots of problem areas. These problems need to be specifically recorded, for example, stains on carpets or existing holes in walls.

Also, make sure they clearly have details noted like the property address, the date of inspection, the rooms and any comments to identify the problem, and signatures of all parties, including an initial on each page.

Top Tip: With residential lets, these can be an unexpected additional charge by the letting agent, which you need to understand from the start. You could look at completing this yourself, although make sure these are done thoroughly and correctly; the agent may explain more or you can search out other examples.

Dilapidations

This has to do with how a property is left after an occupier has vacated as well as still being in occupation. Theoretically, they should have carried out any repairs before they left and handed back the property in tip-top condition. In reality, though, whether deliberate or not, this often isn't the case, in which case the landlord or owner will need to prepare a to-do list of repairs called a Schedule of Dilapidations.

Because the occupier has often left the property, they will have no rights to go back in and do these now, so the gist of these dilapidations can be to agree on a payment to reflect what the new owner or occupier then needs to do in order to carry them out. These can get complicated, particularly with larger and commercial properties, and can include other costs such as VAT, advisors, and even loss of potential income and rent whilst these are being carried out.

Whilst it can sound like an opportunity for a landlord to come up with an endless list of repairs for the property, these do still have to be sensible and can be capped to the actual loss in value of the property and can even be reduced to nothing if it can be shown that the landlord was going to redevelop the property anyway and all these minor repairs are in effect going to be wasted.

Also, check if any deposit can be used to pay towards agreed dilapidation costs at the end of an agreement.

Repairs Notice

Repairs notices are more common in business properties, but these can be in long residential leases as well. These clauses are along the lines of the landlord being able to inspect the property to check what the condition is and to send a formal notice to the tenant to then get on with these repairs. If they don't in a certain time frame, then the landlord has the right to enter the property and carry repairs out themselves and then charge the costs back to the tenant.

The wording of this will need careful checking, including the ability to easily recharge the money as a debt through the lease, and bear in mind that it's often most effective to get an occupier into action rather than needing to carry it through to the bitter end.

Decorations

You can be caught out here because although a property may look okay and not in desperate need of decorations, there can be strict ways in which it needs to be carried out both inside and outside every few years, particularly with business leases. This will probably have to be in a proper manner with two coats and preparation work beforehand and within a certain time frame.

It's therefore critical to get this not only clarified but practically understood by all parties involved.

Liabilities

Remember that others may have a liability for the condition of a property and therefore an obligation to resolve if there are problems. A classic example is through warranties and guarantees, whether direct with, say, a builder, through an external body like NHBC for residential, or a contractor's own liability insurance. This needs to be crystal clear in how it's passed on to other parties to be involved, if need be, not just originally set up.

There are also other indirect responsibilities, for example, the Defective Premises Act 1972, which can help a tenant or occupier pursue, for example, an original builder who did works at the property they were not directly involved with but have a duty for, say, workman and professional manner works to a dwelling so it is fit for habitation.

Top Tip: Always maintain a record of when you inspect a property, including general visits as well as formal assessments, and any other non-repair issues. Even if resolved, jot it all down, and if you have someone else doing this, like a co-tenant or managing agent, then make sure they do this as well.

Landlord Focus: In most cases, the tenant will have a duty to keep the property well repaired, which is good news; however, you need to be aware of the procedures needed and things like inventories, and that you don't get carried away and start assuming things should be improved when in actual fact the tenant is only obliged to repair them. In this case it may be worth liaising with the tenant to come to a compromise where they make a contribution for you to do whatever permanent repair or replacement you want. Also, watch for any indirect opportunity through the service charge or direct charges to pass some of these costs to the tenant.

Investor Focus: It's important to first asses the true condition of the property and then who is liable for these under the leases and agreements. Remember, though, to also assess how this will work in real life. As an example, although a tenant may on paper need to carry out lots of repairs, if they are facing bankruptcy, then this liability may fall back on you as the property owner, or you may find that only certain types of repairs can be recharged back to occupiers when in actual fact you need to look at more substantial repairs in order to make the property relettable in the future and cost effective long term.

Tenant Focus: Be careful what you first sign up for and how this is recorded. Watch how you practically occupy the property as you can suddenly see lots of issues then come to light when you leave the property, for example, scuff marks on walls or scratches on wooden floors.

34. Tenant & Landlord Defaults

Key Points: When your tenant or landlord defaults or does not comply with the terms of the lease, here are the issues you need to be aware of:

- *Arrears*
- *Non-arrears*
- *Other sources*
- *Insolvency*
- *Landlord defaults*

Arrears

Tenant arrears is the most common default, mainly with rent but also any extras such as service charge, insurance premiums, and any additional charges. For residential property, there is greater protection and procedures to go through, making separate advice necessary to make sure things are done correctly.

With short-term occupation and the popular AST (Assured Shorthold Tenancy) agreements, the popular and more realistic way is to look at gaining possession back from the tenant by chasing arrears through court, although you can look at a direct debt recovery through a small claims court application. With these AST agreements, you can serve both Section 8 and Section 21 notices on the tenant with a formal rent arrears letter and rent schedule and then reminder letters.

A Section 21 notice is often better with a Fixed Term or Periodic type, to be served before the fixed term ends with at least two months written notice but after the agreement is signed and deposit secured (there's also Standard and Accelerated Possession Procedures). A Section 8 can be served anytime with up to two months' notice dependant upon ground(s) sought, even during the Fixed Term, provided there is a forfeiture clause in the agreement stating specific grounds for doing this.

Top Tip: Even though a landlord may have a legitimate and mandatory ground to terminate, such as rent arrears under Section 8, the tenant may have a separate counter claim that could be set off against these arrears to mean less actual final payment.

You will then have a Possession Order from the court followed by a Warrant for Possession, if the tenant has not left by the ordered date, and maybe involving a hearing. After this, the landlord may use the court bailiff to evict the tenant, although the tenant may be able to apply to court to suspend action and delay matters.

Top Tip: As well as getting notices technically correct, make sure they're sent in the right way according to the tenancy agreement, usually in person or post, and get proof of doing this.

For commercial property, you have the right of Commercial Rent Arrears Recovery (CRAR) under the Tribunal Courts & Enforcement Act 2007 and the Taking Control of Goods Regulations 2013. In 2014 this replaced the previous principle of distress, which involved bailiffs turning up to a property to begin a process of seizing tenant's goods to pay the arrears. CRAR has similar principles but not quite as drastic consequences; it is only for pure commercial property with no residential part, only for fixed rent excluding anything like service charges or insurance premiums even if labelled or even part of an all-inclusive rent (but includes VAT and interest on the rent), and can only be carried out by a Certified Enforcement Agent.

They must serve an initial notice of enforcement with a minimum seven days' notice after the due-debt (excluding Sundays and bank holidays) and then a Controlled Goods Agreement agreed after they visit the premises to place a legal right over the tenant's goods while an agreed payment plan for arrears is secured, excluding goods that are exempt.

This also brought in changes for involving subtenants with main tenant arrears. Where CRAR is applicable for the main tenant, notice can be served on the subtenant to entitle the landlord to receive the subtenants rent straight to them, failing which after 14 days of the notice the landlord can also apply CRAR action on the subtenant (additional notices needed for future arrears).

The popular method, of course, is court proceedings, although this method through the courts is generally slower and costlier, including being hit with the other side's costs and having less control over the process. A claim form and particulars of claim will need to be served on the defendant debtor, providing them 14 or 28 days to serve a defence depending on whether an acknowledgement of service is filed. If no defence is filed, a judgement in default can be sought or a summary judgement. If not, the court will determine the next steps to resolve, including exchange of evidence, a trial, and noting any counter claim from the debtor.

Another angle with arrears is to look at forfeiting and ending the lease because of these arrears, particularly with commercial property and long residential leases. Some words of caution though: this can mean literally changing the locks and keeping tenants out with commercial property rent arrears, but there needs to be set timescales and action by the landlord so they don't waive their right to do this. The tenant also has a right of relief afterwards if they pay everything and have the lease reinstated back, plus you may not want the tenant to actually leave, just pay arrears.

Non-Arrears

For other tenant breaches of the lease, you'll need to involve solicitors to take action on this, which can involve forfeiture again but only through certain notices and action.

It can be a little more ambiguous here and open to interpretation as to what a breach of the lease is, plus you have to consider what actual loss you have incurred and how you want this resolved; for example through a tenant taking correct action now, money compensation for damages, or the lease ending and the tenant leaving.

Other Sources

You need to know other angles and parties you can call upon if you do have defaults, more commonly when you have arrears, but it may also possibly be for other issues.

Firstly, check if there are any other monies you can use instead, often in the form of a deposit that is held separately and can be drawn upon and then topped-up later by the party in default.

Secondly, see if anybody else can fulfil these obligations, for example, a guarantor or co-tenant. This can include previous commercial tenants that are still guaranteeing and on the hook either through the legal principle of

Privity of Contract for old leases pre-1996 or through an agreed Authorised Guarantee Agreement (AGA) for new leases (check out the Landlord & Tenant Act 1995).

You will then need to look at serving notices under section 17 to alert the former commercial tenant or guarantor of your intention to recover fixed charge arrears of rent, service charge, insurance rent, or any other liquidated sums under the lease (and state if any need to be determined later).

These must be within six months of the charge being due and repeated for future instances of due amounts, plus if the former tenant or guarantor does pay these, they then have a right to request the landlord to grant them an overriding lease to take control of the property back and deal with the old lease or any new ones accordingly.

Insolvency

This is a complex area looking at the technicalities of someone being 'insolvent' and the forms and consequences this can then take, for example personal bankruptcy, administration, liquidation, receivership, and voluntary agreements.

A few pointers though—firstly, you need to understand the correct legal entity on the lease and their true position, taking advice as needed. Sometimes these insolvency situations will suddenly happen; other times they can be forced, and you can end up with, for example, a company going into administration but another company then being reformed and being run by essentially the same people. Be careful, then, of other names that suddenly appear, for example, payment from a slightly different name.

Secondly, look at what other security you can fall back on—maybe a rent deposit or a separate guarantor under the lease that you can call upon to begin paying, maybe even a former tenant as well.

Thirdly, be clear on how you should treat an insolvency situation. Sometimes a party in this position can be immune to normal action and have the protection of a moratorium over them, meaning you need the consent of a court or administrator to do anything else.

Fourthly, look at how you need to split any due arrears to be paid. They often fall into historic arrears up until the point of insolvency plus those that are now due during insolvency, which may be covered under say administration as a genuine expense of the entity still trading at the premises whilst the administrators deal with the assets of the company.

And fifthly, carefully consider if you can serve a statutory procedure on the other side as a preliminary step to pursuing bankruptcy in the case of an individual or winding up and liquidation in the case of a company. So this is where they owe you money and you're now instigating their financial end in order to release your payment. The debt must be at least £750 and liquidated and undisputed, and you must allow the debtor 21 days after service to settle up, after which a bankruptcy or winding-up petition can be presented to the court.

This can be a quick process, but drastic, so take legal advice, and remember that even if successful, you will rank as an unsecured creditor in the end bankruptcy or liquidation, and trustees in bankruptcy or liquidations do have power to disclaim and get out of any property interest anyway.

Top Tip: The golden rule is to check the actual viability and financial status of the party with the default as soon as possible. Carry out searches, and check if they're still solvent and, if so, if they have any assets and finances to actually pay their arrears or remedy their breaches. If not, a lot of efforts and costs of pursuing will be wasted.

Landlord Defaults

For tenants, who are the ones in the property paying the landlord, there are situations when the landlord can also be in default. Maybe they owe money for repairs, or there was an agreed rent-free, or they are not doing their part under the lease or not allowing the tenant to get on with things (known as 'quiet enjoyment').

As mentioned in the payments section, often the tenant is not allowed to deduct monies from the rent they pay, with setoff not being permitted under the lease. It's then often down to taking legal advice or with the case of residential property, going to authorities like the First-Tier Tribunal (Property Chamber – Residential Property) for advice and action.

Top Tip: Landlords who sell their property need to be careful that they are still not on the hook through the lease with a tenant even though a former landlord has nothing to do with the property. There is a procedure to release this through the Landlord & Tenant (Covenants) Act 1995, and there should really be a clause in the lease specifically excluding this anyway, which will need checking.

Landlord Focus: Rent arrears will be the big issue to watch out for, so keep an eye on things. Always try open talks first, but be careful of this going nowhere and sometimes hindering action later on.

Investor Focus: Try to determine if there are any bad patterns of payment or behaviour from tenants as these can prove to be a hassle and cost in the future, plus this could be reflected in any valuations and the covenant strength of the tenants.

Tenant Focus: Keep on top of payments and issues with the landlord to save them needing to look at further action, and keep in good communication with them as this is half the battle. When you have issues with the landlord yourself, then carefully consider what, legally, you are able to do about it.

35. Notices

Key Points: Notices are often needed for formal communication under a lease or agreement; therefore, they need to be correct in order to make sure they're effective. Here are the main issues to consider:

- *The right procedure*
- *The right receipt*
- *The right follow-up*

The Right Procedure

First check what it says in the whole lease or other documentation regarding notices for a variety of reasons, for example, towards the end of the lease, exercising a right in the lease or sale document, making sure a break option in actioned, or triggering and dealing with a rent review. It may say what needs doing, in what way and format, in whatever time frame, to whomever.

Secondly, check what any legislation says as there may be very specific templates to use that possibly only a solicitor can serve. Legislation can also help as a fall-back position on what good practice is if there isn't enough detail in the lease or agreement or where any 'reasonableness' needs be applied.

The Right Receipt

After you have clarified the correct way to serve notice, make sure it is effectively received by whoever needs it. If by post, then use recorded delivery. If emails, then make sure there is no bounce back. If fax, then get a record of it going through properly. The secret is to have evidence of it effectively being recognised by others.

There are two little tricks to help with this. The first is to allow for any delays, particularly with post delays that can occur, and excluding, for example, Sundays, for it to be sent. Secondly, send copies if you're in doubt of where it needs to go, so the document may need to be sent to the head office of a company, but it may be worthwhile sending (and recording) a copy to the actual property address or their representative as well.

Top Tip: When you're issuing urgent payment, make sure you have a record of it being sent and ideally clearing, whether it's a printout from online banking or a receipt from your bank.

The Right Follow-up

Once you've sent or received notice, be careful about how you react to this as it may be in your best interests to either immediately recognise or deliberately ignore. One example for which there has been lots of activity in court cases is when a break option is actioned in a lease, as a landlord can have difficulty in claiming that it is invalid if they acknowledge receipt and the consequences of it. Be careful not to get so friendly with the other party, even if things are being agreed perfectly well, and make sure correct notices and communication are still sent.

Landlord Focus: Remember that leases do offer protection to tenants so make sure notices are served and received correctly and are clearly documented.

Investor Focus: You need to be careful how these are carried out if they are out of your direct control and how other parties, such as managing agents and solicitors, behave. Also check historical issues, and if previous matters have or have not been notified, including written evidence of this.

Tenant Focus: As well as considering any that you need to issue, be careful about any that you receive yourself from the landlord or any other authorities, such as the local planning authority, where you may be obliged under your lease to forward this to your landlord.

36. Land Titles & Rights

Key Points: The official land title not only applies to when you own land and property freehold but all other kinds of rights and leases that affect you and others. Here's a quick overview of what to consider:

- *Land registry*
- *Registered ownership*
- *Registered rights*
- *Plans*

Land Registry

You've probably heard of the Land Registry, which is the government agency that registers all land interests in the country, with one of the most important and recent pieces of legislation affecting property being the Land Registration Act 2002. So if you own a piece of land, then it will probably have a unique reference and be noted with the Land Registry on a central database.

The important thing to realise is that this isn't necessarily to do with the actual legal ownership of any land or other property interest, such as a long lease. Your ownership will depend upon a legally-applicable transaction and document, such as a deed or lease, and there is, in fact, still unregistered and often older pieces of land that although they may not be registered yet with Land Registry, they are still legally owned by someone.

It can cause problems, though, where things should be registered and they are not. You can get different expressions of ownership and title not necessarily being guaranteed or absolute. In short, you need to make sure interests are officially registered by the Land Registry as an important log that you may need to rely on later, and this includes leases over seven years and other agreements other than usual freehold land ownership.

This can then help at points like a sale, for at this point of transaction there is a new legal owner; however, it can take weeks or even months for the new owner to be registered with the Land Registry. There can be clauses in the lease and sales agreement obliging someone to do this quickly and pay any Land Registry administration fees.

Top Tip: You can access land title details for plots of land along with plans and other reports, such as flood surveys, from the land registry website for charges under £10. These are handy to obtain knowledge regarding your own and neighbouring property quickly.

Registered Ownership

So registered ownership will tend to fall into two areas: the freehold title, and long leases more than seven years old. On these title details, there will be information such as when it was last transacted, at what price, and previous owners.

There is also something called adverse possession, which, in short, means that if someone actually uses a property other than the true owner for 12 years, then they can actually claim the title ownership themselves. It sounds too good to be true, gaining a freehold title effectively for free, and, of course, there is criteria to comply with such as notices to the current registered owner, but this is something to be aware of with older and unused or unknown and unregistered pieces of land.

Registered Rights

This is when things get complicated and you hear terms like easements, restrictions, and covenants with the land. In short, this is where others may have a right to use your piece of land for some reason, such as access or utility/service cables stretching across or drain runs, and also vice versa where you have the same rights over other pieces of land.

You need to focus on three things here. Firstly, what rights already exist in any registered or unregistered titles, and if any separate documents exist. This will mean wading through documentation you have or that is registered with the Land Registry, with an expert's help to clearly explain.

Secondly, you need to consider how land and property is being used now and previously, ideally over the last 20 years at least, to see if any rights have been implied or prescribed over time that you didn't release. This can be particularly important for other less obvious rights as well as such rights of lights and support with adjacent buildings that can be costly mistakes to sort out afterwards.

Thirdly, you need to be ready to take further action where needed, maybe further surveys or special reports. If there is no easy way to get answers, then you could even look at special title insurance to help cover you in case any issues are ever raised with, say, your neighbours.

In extreme cases, you can also apply to a relevant Tribunal to have old, unnecessary, and outdated restrictions actually removed from the title, with one example from many years ago of a property being built and occupied as a bank but having a restriction in the land to say it could never change. There was no market demand for another bank, and a restaurant use was the only realistic alternative, which was strong enough grounds to request a release through the Land Tribunal, although in these circumstances, a solution was able to be negotiated with the neighbouring land owner, who benefited from this particular restriction.

Top Tip: If you have confusing or unknown rights, then it may be worth negotiating with whomever to come to a resolution and then agree a document to clarify and then register with Land Registry. Access over a path or other driveway can be a classic example that has happened for many years and suddenly gets spotted when being sold.

Plans

Pay attention to plans and, in particular, boundaries on them. They may not necessarily match the reality of what is used on the land or what's in the rest of the title, and this will need to be clarified. The general boundaries principle by the Land Registry is that the red line on the plan is not definite and only provides a general indication of the actual legal boundary. Even a 1 mm red line on a Land Registry plan (green ones are excluded land) on a 1:1250 scale translates to 1.25m on site, which can be a key area.

If there are still uncertainties then check any pre-registration deeds or, failing this, the actual physical boundary on site, like walls, hedges, and fences, and even the conduct of property owners.

The Land Registry also has powers to determine a boundary more accurately under the Land Registration Act 2002, or you could come to voluntary agreement with your neighbour, which although won't change the Land Registry plan boundary, it can be a registered agreement with the land title.

Plans also need to now be a certain type in order to be registered with the Land Registry, so you may find that you need to arrange new ones rather than try to use older ones. You can arrange a specialist surveyor to do these or search online and purchase through means such as Ordinance Survey.

Landlord Focus: Make sure your title matches what you plan to grant to a tenant or purchaser and that anything that needs to be registered with the Land Registry is completed. Be clear on whether this is yours or the tenant's responsibility.

Investor Focus: Solicitors will carry out due diligence and replies to enquires when you're looking at taking on an investment. Try to receive all this information as soon as possible, and make sure it matches reality at the property, spot things that may be amiss, and, if need be, look at insurance cover being taken out.

Tenant Focus: Make sure your lease or other side documents are registered, if need be, and do your own land title searches even if quickly online to see if things make sense and that your landlord has the ability to grant what they are proposing through your lease.

37. The Law

Key Points: Knowing 'the law' in property management and, in fact, any subject is huge. Here are a few angles to remember and how they apply to property:

- *Legislation basis*
- *Implications*
- *Residential property*

Legislation Basis

We all have the law of the land governing how we live; therefore, the best way to look at this in the context of property management is firstly the general law that applies to everyone, irrespective of any property interest. So there is criminal law governing how someone breaks into a property and causes damage, there is the principle of causing a nuisance to another person, there is also the principle of being negligent to another person if you have a duty to them to do or provide something, and there can be general contract law and the law of tort.

Employment law and contracts may also be applicable when dealing with individuals directly, for example, contractors and managing agents, and there is general legislation regarding how others are treated; for example, it is unlawful for any organisation involved in housing or residential property to discriminate on racial grounds.

There's also company law, which will affect the establishment and operation of management companies, for example, and the way that parties such as landlords and tenants are treated. All of these have an indirect effect on property just like any other area of life.

Secondly, there will be pieces of legislation applicable to property in particular; particularly with residential property and the protection of people, but also to the way property is transacted and paid for, and to the practical maintenance and running of it.

Thirdly, there are pieces of legislation that can apply when a very specific contract or arrangement is in place with someone at a property, for example, leases and licences, or there may be an obligation implied in most cases for landlords to act reasonably in leases, not just by general law principles but under a specific statute.

Implications

Okay, let's take a step back. You don't need to know all the details of the law here. The secret is to know what angles and different pieces of legislation may need to be looked at. With property management, you're dealing with lots of areas of law, and to some degree, you need to be always thinking of the wider picture and asking questions.

So firstly, do your own swatting up. Read up, do online research, and get helpful guides on the main pieces of legislation, but keep it general. Secondly, involve others that should know the detail and implication here, not only solicitors but maybe surveyors that specialise in applying this to real-life property. It could also be any general regulatory bodies and any general guides or requirements they adhere to.

Thirdly, take a conscious step back to question things and make sure you get to the bottom line. Keep asking 'why'. Why can't a tenant or landlord take this action? Come up with some crazy ideas, knowing that it may never happen, but it will force clear thinking anyway. Also be aware of any other ad-hoc pieces of legislation that can suddenly apply in a particular situation.

Top Tip: Remember to consider legislation that may also be applicable to individual parties involved and how they in particular deal with your property interest, for example, the Charities Act 2011 if you're involved with a charity yourself or the other party is a registered charity and the notices that may have to be served or received as well as additional reports being carried out.

Residential Property

With the management of long leasehold residential property, there are five pieces of legislation in particular affecting it; the Landlord & Tenant Act 1988 and 1987, the Leasehold Reform, Housing & Urban Development Act 1993, the Housing Act 1996, and the Commonhold & Leasehold Reform Act 2002.

As an example in terms of what rights these provide, first there is the statutory right for two or more leaseholders to request an independent management audit if they are suspicious about the accounting and documentation at the property, under the Leasehold Reform, Housing, & Urban Development Act 1993.

Secondly, any party under Section 35 of the Landlord & Tenant Act 1987 can apply to a Tribunal to actually have the terms in a lease legally changed if there are not a 'satisfactory provision', for example, to do with repairs, insurance, and monies.

Thirdly, 'qualifying tenants' have a right to first buy the freehold if the landlord is selling as a 'relevant disposal' under the Landlord & Tenant Act 1987. This can have consequences on previous sales for others not already going through this process, which won't invalidate any sale but rather cause rights by the leaseholder against both the old and new owners. Also, there may be ways to structure a transfer through, say, selling a holding company, not the actual freehold, which excludes this obligation on the landlord. The landlord must first serve a Section 5 notice on each qualifying tenant, and tenants an acceptance notice in the right way and timescale.

Fourthly, as already mentioned in this book, there is a right for leaseholders to purchase the freehold, known as enfranchisement, which is different to the above point in that it can be pursued by the leaseholders at any time if the criteria is right rather than just when the landlord is selling. This can be a joint exercise for multiple tenants in a block of flats (collective enfranchisement) or individually for a single house under a different piece of legislation, the Leasehold Reform Act 1967.

When it's collective, there will be conditions such as minimum number of tenants on long leases and limited commercial elements. If successful, the tenants will need to pay a premium to the landlord for the freehold, determined by a Tribunal if it can't be negotiated with a statutory formula along the lines of the market value plus 50% of the 'marriage value' for unexpired leases of 80 years or less (i.e., the extra value from the freehold and leasehold interests having the same control). Where both a head and subtenant have a right to enfranchise, the subtenant's right takes priority.

Number five, there is a formal Right To Manage (RTM) and, number six, a right to long lease extensions, both detailed in other sections of this book.

Number seven, there's a right for service charges to be fair and reasonable and set procedures to be met regarding unusual recurring or one-off expenditure detailed in the earlier payment perspective.

Number eight, in a similar fashion, any administration charges also need to be fair and reasonable with the ability of both parties to apply to a Tribunal to determine this. These tend to include costs outlined in the lease, such as landlord costs, for dealing with any assignments and sales and can include more generic costs, such as replying to a purchaser's enquires, which tend to just be agreed between the parties.

Landlord Focus: You have to be particularly clued up here as tenants will generally have a lot of protection, and even though the principles of eviction or chasing arrears are correct, unless it has gone under a proper procedure and is compliant with general law, you can hit big problems later on.

Investor Focus: As well as legislation regarding the property, consider the law around yourself and the entity that holds the property in terms of regulations, company law, and how you need to behave.

Tenant Focus: Know your rights, but also know how they need to be appropriately applied. There will be a lot of helpful guides and support services around to help you with whatever areas are needed or simply good general overviews.

38. Marketing & Communication

Key Points: Marketing and advertising property does need careful documentation in order to clarify everything, so here is what to look out for:

- *The theory*
- *The details*
- *The security*
- *The extras*
- *The DIY approach*

The Theory

When you're dealing with a transaction in property like a sale or letting, you're dealing with big issues both in terms of values involved and potential problems that could emerge. There is, therefore, quite rightly a raft of documentation to be aware of that is designed to protect all parties involved: the owners, any tenants, the third parties like estate agents who are involved in the advertising and selling, and those looking to buy or rent.

Different angles are therefore covered. The information being given about the property must be accurate, the procedure for making offers clear and the opportunities for late ones known, the organisation of monies safe, the protection of people's data strong, and the role of everyone involved clarified. Do some research as there are often good guides around, and don't be afraid to ask those involved, as transparency should quite rightly be the focus.

There are three levels of documentation to be aware of with all of this. The first is general legislation, which can get complicated and fragmented. The Estate Agent Act 1979 and Property Misdescription Act are two older examples, but there's also the Unfair Terms in Consumer Contracts Regulations, plus the Freedom of Information Act and the Data Protection Act.

This includes the nature of any negotiations and final agreed terms, so, for example, you may need specific clauses in agreements like leases and management agreements and procedures in place to ensure no party has been enticed and bribed unfairly under the Bribery Act 2010 through rent concessions and abatements, fit-out contributions, contractors' agreements, and corporate hospitality.

The second is the regulation of any particular party in the transaction, typically more the middle parties like estate agents and surveyors. They may be part of an accredited scheme or have additional regulation just for that sector.

The third is then the actual contract and terms and conditions that you sign up to for your property transaction.

The Details

Always check the actual details about the property or particulars to make sure they're accurate, have all the official terms in them, and at the same time are looking great and catching people's eyes, including lots of photos and genuinely helpful information. Provide lots of ways to contact, including maybe even a totally separate website or even Facebook page all about the property interest and any unique aspects, such as providing block viewings.

The Security

Remember that as soon as you're holding and dealing with any personal data like even a tenant's number on your phone or you pass to another party like the Home Office with immigration checks, you'll have an obligation to keep it safe, including registration with the Information Commissioners Office (ICO).

The Extras

There are a few other angles you'll need to be aware of, one being the issues surrounding the use of letting and for-sale boards on properties. This involves planning issues as well as looking at what information they have on them.

Also, watch out for when you involve several parties in the mix and what they often call 'joint agency'. So if you have two estate agents selling your property, be clear on how the fee/commissions are split and how things work out if things get messy. So one agency may claim they found the eventual buyer, whereas the second one says they actually took the initial enquiry.

Also make sure that anyone that needs to give consent to the sale or letting has done so, for example, joint owners, lenders, insurers, guarantors, superior landlords and freeholders, and local authorities.

Plus, watch out for any non-essential issues and services emerging that simply aren't needed. You could easily get carried away with extra things like mail shots, additional newspaper adverts, and packs of blurb, when in actual fact these may not pay off. Sometimes, though, they can, so if your property would suit a particular type of person, for example a business with similar retail shops in the area, where I've seen it work well when you simply contact them about your opportunity.

Estate and letting agencies may also try to bring in their other services, such as property management and costs for renewing leases, when in actual fact you don't need them or at least need to look at other options rather than default to this one.

The DIY Approach

To some degree, get involved yourself. So even if you have others doing everything, still check and oversee things to make sure nothing is missed and things don't get carried away. The world of advertising can get a little vague, and it's good to keep grounded with real results emerging, and yourself, with the most at stake and who's paying the bill, is the best person to spot this.

If you do more yourself, then look at obvious things like simple signs outside the property and adverts online as well as offline. This is where agents can have the advantage as they have accounts with larger websites with properties on there that do capture a lot of interest nowadays.

Also look at good old word of mouth. Ask around to neighbours and even existing tenants, offer an incentive to them for finding another tenant, and pop an advert up in your local shops. Newspaper and related-publication adverts can also be good, but be careful as they can be a poor return on your cost. Trial it, and maybe put a unique website address on there for people to go to as there are ways nowadays to track how many people then actually click on this to see how many people came to it from this particular advert.

Landlord Focus: Try to get involved yourself even when using others, begin looking at things earlier rather than later, and carefully plan. If you're providing a good service already to existing tenants, then maybe try the DIY word-of-mouth approach as well.

Investor Focus: If you're looking to sell or buy an investment, you may have to actually keep advertisements under the radar. Existing occupiers may get upset if they know this, so no blatant signs or adverts may be needed, and viewings kept discrete.

Tenant Focus: Know your rights as you look for a property, and consider different options. If you're looking for other lodgers or occupiers yourself, then you will need to look at it from a landlord's perspective as well.

39. Planning

Key Points: Planning permission will often come into play with any changes to a building, so these are the areas to consider:

- *The principles*
- *The practice*
- *Lawful Development Certificates*
- *Other areas*

The Principles

You'll have undoubtedly heard of planning permission as it's such a notable issue within the UK when it comes to property and one of the major issues surrounding how quickly we are building new homes and properties in the UK. It's the way in which the government has its say on any changes to a building in terms of how much space is being carried out or type of design.

On one side, it's about 'building changes'. So any kind of new building, extension, or major facelift to a property or piece of land may fall into the need for planning permission, although there are some works automatically allowable under a General Permitted Development Order.

Top Tip: Don't underestimate just what changes need planning permission, no matter how small you think they are. Two examples are a retail shop installing any illuminated signage and air conditioning units, which can require this.

On the other side, it can involve just the use of the property needing planning permission, whether or not you're making any physical changes at the same time. There are set 'Use Classes' under the Planning Use Classes Order, the general rule being that if your new use falls within the same category or certain others, often below the list, then you don't need permission, whereas if different, then you do. This is a huge area, and it can have a massive effect on the value of the property and its ability to be used for other uses under planning restrictions, irrespective of what any lease says.

The Practice

You need to apply for planning permission with your local authority through a planning application. This can involve separate reports and information depending upon its complexity, and there is a set time frame for this to be determined by the planners after consultation with others, for example, your neighbours by letter and notice at the property. If it's a no, then there are rights of an appeal. It could be a straight yes, or yes with conditions for the types of works or construction, or trading hours of any new uses.

Once permission is granted, then works actually need to start to reflect this permission within three years from the date of grant unless stated otherwise, or the permission lapses and you need to reapply.

If you carry out works or uses, deliberately or not, and you breach planning permissions, you may get planners contacting you informally to resolve or a more formal Enforcement Notice, which means changes have got to be made in a set time or further action will be taken.

Two pieces of advice here: Firstly, make sure you get the timing right, particularly if you're trying to sort out any changes to the building. So allow time to get this permission and sort out issues before building works start, or refrain from agreeing a new lease without knowing whether a new use or refit works are allowed.

Secondly, enter early dialogue with planners or advisors to see how the land lies. You can speak with a Planning Officer at the council and have an informal discussion on the merits of your proposal or even your neighbours if you know that they're going to possibly have negative feedback.

You can research what factors may determine this, so look at previous applications in the area online or the planning documents and guides that will be used to consider applications. Even involve a planning consultant to make sure you get this right from the start and approach it in the correct way. It may be a suitable application in principle, but it has to be presented and worded in the right way.

Lawful Development Certificates

This is where a use has been happening for a period of time, and you can apply for a certificate to confirm that it is permitted at the moment with no need therefore for a planning application to change any use, a classic example being using a piece of spare land for a temporary carpark.

Other Areas

There are other related issues with planning to consider, such as Listed Building consent, which is technically not a planning issue but uses similar principles. This is where a building is designated as of special interest, probably because of historic interest and needing protection, where you'll need to apply for listed building consent for any changes in addition to planning permission.

On a similar line, you have designed Conservation Areas in the country that trigger further planning controls, or there can be other special planning designed areas.

In terms of other related areas, but not directly part of the main planning system, there is a right to designate land as a Town or Village Green (TVG) for the public interest and use for sports and pastimes, therefore restricting any future development opportunities for the landowner.

Another example is Assets of Community Value (ACV) under the Localism Act 2011, where communities can identify a building or piece of land they believe is important to their community's social well-being with a right to buy it at a fair market value if it comes up for sale.

Landlord Focus: Don't only think about what change you way want for the property in the short and long term but also what a potential new occupier might want. It may be worth you applying now so it's good-to-go and can attract a new tenant.

Investor Focus: As well as looking at what future permissions are needed, check that existing uses or changes have permission already as it may come back and bite if not.

Tenant Focus: If you're planning any kind of use or material change to the building, this may apply, so look into it carefully. You'll need to check the timing and involve the landlord anyway as they will be notified of any applications as the building owner. Plus, leases often state that you need to communicate any planning issues to them.

40. Highways

Key Points: Having designated areas of land under highways control can be more involved than what you first think. Here's what you need to note:

- *Determine the situation*
- *Determine any changes*

Determine the Situation

The Highways Agency have designated areas of land under their remit to maintain, through the local authority, in order to make sure the main routes for traffic in the country are up to a high standard. As well as actual roadways, it includes areas such as pavements or small yard areas, walkways, etc.

Try to get to the bottom of things by determining the degree to which the land is controlled or even owned by the council. In terms of how such public rights of way and dedication of routes as a highway come about, this can be through adoption of a new road/highway by the Highway Authority under the Highways Act 1980, or by appropriate use.

Firstly, agree in black and white what the status quo is at the moment and then any changes that need making. Sift through any highways agreements and any other documentation, plans, and notices to clarify this, and contact the local authority or Highways Agency for more clarity.

Then liaise with them to agree on the nitty-gritty detail of what they are actually maintaining and dealing with as a lot of times it can be a great advantage for a landowner to have this being done for them, although sometimes it can be difficult when there needs to be changes or improvements to this land and the authority may cause delays or frustrations with this.

Determine Any Changes

Secondly, be careful of the timing with new designations, a classic example being with a new housing estate and the access roads only being taken on by Highways after everything is completed. This can take longer and should include pavements and also street lighting. The original developer and owner have to keep maintaining these in the meantime, although often to the bare minimum and maybe not even with a top-surface of tarmac on the roads yet.

Thirdly, watch out for pieces of land becoming designated that you don't want to, particularly through presumed use for 20 years or over shorter periods of time in some situations. Look at regularly closing routes off, erecting visible notices, or even a procedure under Section 31(6) of the 1980 Act to deposit a map of land at the appropriate council.

And fourthly, watch out for the extent of such ownership, including the boundaries and what additional pavements, etc., are included.

Landlord Focus: Clarify this on any land you have, making sure responsibilities don't clash with any demised areas you give to tenants. Likewise, also help clarify with occupiers who is responsible for what.

Investor Focus: These details must really be established on paper and any uncertainties clarified. This can have an effect on the running costs of the property and the ability to carry out any changes and redevelopment of the scheme, hence having an eventual impact on your investment value.

Tenant Focus: Although it won't necessarily affect you directly, check out any access areas and who's dealing with what and, as above, particularly with any changes and new designations, how quickly and effectively these will actually occur.

41. Party Walls

Key Points: *This is a separate obligation regarding shared 'party' walls, which can easily be missed or misunderstood. Here are the main points to remember:*

- *The general gist*
- *Gaining agreement*

The General Gist

It's determined by a piece of legislation called the Party Wall etc. Act 1996, which outlines a procedure needed for works to certain types of walls and structures at a building. This is separate to usual building issues, such as planning permission or building control, and can be easily missed by those not aware of it. It is sometimes seen on TV programmes and people renovating residential properties unawares of this obligation with their neighbours.

The idea is simple. Any part of your building that joins or affects a neighbouring property means there could be damage to your neighbour's building when you do works. This is therefore a safeguard for you to officially notify and involve them to make sure such 'works' are agreed.

It includes party walls, boundaries, and any excavation works near neighbouring buildings. There's details available on what specific works actually fall within this in the various free guides, so see if this relates to your work. The trick here, though, is to look through carefully, check the total works involved, quiz any builder or surveyor involved in your works, and prepare for worst-case scenarios.

An example might be a basement that you're converting to a kitchen area, and suddenly you're in the realm of needing to dig the floor level down farther, which may fall within this need to notify your neighbouring property if you're in a terraced property.

Gaining Agreement

If you are covered by this legislation, then the next stage is to notify your neighbours of your plans as per procedures under the Act. The neighbours can then agree or disagree; if the latter, then a procedure for resolving exists, including the appointment of an independent surveyor to help determine. The key here is to be upfront and try to resolve any issues early on, failing which you could be facing notable hassle and costs in dealing with afterwards. Try to resolve even down to the involvement of surveyors and minimising this as you will be the one having to pay the bill as the party instigating this.

On the other side, if you receive a notice or suspect this may affect your own property by your neighbour's work, then ask them for clarity on this in order to determine if these will be okay. Even if you are fine with this, you really need things confirming in writing as any future occupier or owner may ask the same questions.

Landlord Focus: This is essential to consider in any of yours of your tenant's proposed works. It is, of course, easier when you own the property next door anyway, although in case these are separate titles now or in the future it is still worth going through the exercise.

Investor Focus: Make sure this is covered and documented in any building survey carried out or suspected works, both proposed and historic.

Tenant Focus: In most cases, this won't affect you, although this depends upon if you are liable for the structure under your lease. If you are and you're doing major works, then remember that you now need to involve the next-door owner in permission as well as your landlord and other authorities. If not, then watch out for any suspected activity next door that you're worried about, and let your landlord know so that they can look into it.

42. Building Control

Key Points: You may have already heard of phrases like 'building regs' and 'building control' that you need with any large repairs and project works to a property. Here's the basic gist of these:

- *Building control*
- *Other help*

Building Control

Under various building regulations and legislation, you need to gain approval through the local authority for certain project works at properties, the idea being a form of control-check on the workmanship and safety of larger works and for the government to bring in certain parameters, for example, buildings needing to be more 'green' now with greater insulation and fewer CO_2 emissions.

As well as any new works, extensions and new buildings coming underneath these, remember any existing project works and refurbishments being applicable. You'll need to check what 'building regs' apply and then make sure the works are being carried out safely under them.

This can include less obvious 'changes' to the building; for example, you may only be taking down partitions, which in themselves do not need any such approval, but by doing so, you're changing the fire-escape and prevention measures at the property, which may require approval. Another example is repairing a notable part of a roof, which can trigger requirements for certain levels of new insulation.

Other Help

Start off with professionals, surveyors, and good contractors that know the law for general advice over and above your own research. Make sure they can think outside of the box a little, and know other related issues and knock-on effects at the property, not just literally the issues of, say, knocking down a supporting wall.

Secondly, consider a Component Person Scheme, which is where a contractor proves that they already carry out works to a certain standard that are automatically acceptable building-regulation wise rather than you needing to formally apply for building regulation approval for that particular job; for example, window installers, plumbers, or electricians. Make sure they are correctly vetted, that they deal with any local-authority contact that is needed, and that they provide a certificate at the end to confirm compliance.

Thirdly, as well as involving the local authority directly and their building inspectors, you can use an independent Approved Inspector that is already authorised to deal with building control work and be your point of contact to agree any changes. Search for good local ones, and make sure you understand what the service is and the potential issues identified.

Landlord Focus: Keep an eye on any alterations that your tenant is carrying out as well as your own works that may fall within the building control arena.

Investor Focus: Make sure approval is there for any existing works being carried out as well as future ones. Ensure someone has gone through the history of any works at the property both on paper and in reality to check that these exist, as sometimes they can get missed or forgotten at the end of the works.

Tenant Focus: For larger works, you may need this, which will probably require your landlord's knowledge and involvement according to the lease.

43. Contractors

Key Points: Making sure you have the right contractors correctly instructed can not only save you time, cost, and hassle in the future but keep you from any direct liability. Here's what you need to consider:

- *The right choice*
- *The correct documentation*
- *CDM*
- *TUPE*

The Right Choice

Take a step back and work out what you're trying to achieve by using a contractor to then determine how you go about it. It may be a simple job, where you really need as cheap as possible and where you want good, direct contact with the person to make sure they carry it out correctly, in which case finding a local tradesman is probably your answer. On the other side, it could be a larger project that needs to consider lots of issues and complications and may involve building control, in which case you'll need to tender to possibly larger companies, maybe through a professional advisor or project manager and after an initial survey.

Try to balance your instinct with the paperwork. Ask around for a trustworthy contractor, check out reviews and previous examples of work by actually contacting previous clients, and try to meet them face to face to get to the bottom line. But always make sure things are then backed up in writing, for even with the best contractor in the world with the most genuine of intentions, unexpected things can happen, and you may need to resort to what was agreed in black and white.

Top Tip: Check if the actual contractor is doing the work or if they are subcontracting to someone else, or have different individuals working. It's maybe worth asking to meet and speak with the person on the ground actually doing the job or to go straight to the actual contractor rather than subcontracting. Sometimes, though, it can be best to stay with the sub situation as the main contractor can take on the responsibility and liability for organising them, particularly if there are lots of trades involved.

In terms of when you have tradesmen on site, an important lesson is to keep on top of things, particularly when you have multiple ones or it's a complicated project. You unfortunately see this mistake made time and time again on TV renovation programmes with someone buying a property at the other end of the country and simply leaving a main contractor to get on with the works. In reality, there are lots of niggly day-to-day queries to answer and the correct timing of each tradesman to organise and line up with, say, deliveries.

The Correct Documentation

First of all, check if there are any requirements elsewhere for a certain contractor and documentation. A lease might state this, or an insurance policy may insist that an electrician must be so-and-so qualified, or a good-practice guide that your business is part of a certain scheme.

Secondly, do the initial checks to make sure the company is legitimate, which can include references and reviews that not only give you peace of mind but show you've made reasonable investigations. Check if the contractor is a company or an individual, for how long they have been trading, and maybe even a set of accounts to show they are used to dealing with bigger contracts and monies.

Thirdly, check that they are sufficiently covered. This includes the correct employers, professional indemnity, and public liability insurance cover in case of an accident or mistake, being part of an accreditation scheme, and compliance where applicable with HMRC under the Construction Industry Scheme. Also, their agreement to any procedures with the parties or building involved such as equal opportunities and anti-discrimination policies, and then an appropriate contract or terms and conditions, including indemnifying the parties in full against all charges and expenses arising from claims made against them due to the work being carried out.

This may be a legal necessity, maybe with a plumber or electrician with say CORGI or NICEIC; however, bear in mind that there will be limitations to what these schemes can check, meaning you need to do your own due diligence.

Top Tip: A lot of accreditation schemes have online access to their list of contractors so that you can first check that they are members and then search for new ones in your area. Even then, it's still worth contacting the schemes direct to make sure there are no issues.

Thirdly, confirm the actual terms of instruction. This may be in a definite contract, for example, standard JCT Minor Works Contract, which you can easily purchase, standard terms and conditions of the contractor which you have checked, or a written letter with basic terms agreed. Make it as specific as possible to your job, including deadlines, consequences of thing being missed, payments, and payment dates.

Fourthly, make sure the Health & Safety information is in place before they start. There should be a generic Health & Safety document ideally for them as a business explaining how they generally operate and an appropriate person on site to ensure compliance, but then you will need individual documents for your particular job, for example, Risk Assessment or Method Statement (sometimes known as RAMS contained together) and which should include any additional assessments that are appropriate, for example, Working At Height or when a Permit to Work will be issued before any hazardous work. Check the details here and that they make sense, and refer to issues like any change in the weather and how they operate rather than just an off-the-shelf general one.

Top Tip: Any scaffolding must be erected and maintained by appropriately trained and experienced contractors, so if a main contractor is arranging this as a whole project, ensure it's been done by the appropriate parties, with the right documentation and handover certificates and inspection logs. They may also need clear signs and cordoning off tape to ensure they are safely used or walked past by people, along with precautions such as debris netting and even scaffold alarms as they can unfortunately provide people with easy access to parts of the building and site equipment out of hours.

CDM

Large jobs can fall within greater obligations under Construction (Design and Management) Regulations (CDM), as recently revised. Basically, someone has to check that things are going all right, which may involve an external professional or CDM coordinator or possibly a principal contractor to tie it all together.

Top Tip: You may come across the Health & Safety File for a property, which is basically the bible for the building in terms of how it was originally built and is compliant. Most people don't realise it's a legal requirement to have these. So even though you may not need it now, make sure you request it in any sale or letting transaction.

TUPE

Under the Transfer of Undertakings (Protection of Employment) Regulations 2000, as amended by the Collators Redundancies & Transfer of Undertakings (protection of Employment) (Amendment Regulations 2014), otherwise known as TUPE and pronounced as 'tu-pee', these are rights protecting people and their employment, particularly when the organisation or service they work for transfers to a new employer.

So with property, these can be triggered in a property transaction affecting the facilities at that property, maybe the managing agent or regular cleaners, and means that individuals have employment rights and can't simply be terminated along with the service or organisation they're part of. This is a specialised area involving personnel and employment issues you need to check from all different perspectives.

Landlord Focus: These things all need to be considered when you're looking at any kind of works as you'll often be under various obligations by law, the lease, and others, like the insurers.

Investor Focus: Make sure everything that has already been done has been completed correctly and documented as well as looking at future proposals. This includes due diligence when you take on a new investment regarding previous works and issues.

Tenant Focus: As well as taking note of this for your own contractors, use these principles to check who your landlord is using, particularly where you are paying the bill either directly or through a service charge. Check out the names of the contractors as some managing agents can be using their own related company contractors as well, which may be fine, although this needs to be transparent and proven that they are just as competitive and able as any other independent one.

44. Health & Safety

Key Points: 'Health and safety' has turned into a dreaded buzz word in all kinds of areas of life in the UK, so here are the main points concerning property:

- *The range of issues*
- *The arrangement of issues*
- *RIDDOR*

The Range of Issues

The best way to view this is that 'health and safety' covers a range of different issues rather than all being packaged together in one piece of legislation and issue. There are, for example, more general obligations, such as liabilities for a landlord in the Landlord & Tenant Act 1985 and for employers under the Health and Safety at Work etc. Act 1974 or just the common-law principles for landlords and employers.

They boil down to the person in control of the property making sure things are safe for others to use them and will cover all kinds of issues from fire prevention, gas and electricity, water, safe buildings and repairs, safe cleaning and refuse, or security of the property and people within it. The way that all these different aspects are then pieced together on a practical level is in the form of a Risk Assessment, which is basically an analysis of all kinds of issues at a property that may arise with proposed action on how to make sure things like this don't happen and that risks are minimised as far as possible.

The Arrangement of Issues

With a Risk Assessment properly in place, any problem or claim can then be defended by the person in control of the property on the basis that they've done everything they reasonably could have to stop things from happening.

Ways to look at these issues are firstly the practical property issues and secondly the more general process of people using such a property. The practical ones are to do with what you actually need to do to the property to make it safe, so repair that damaged floor so it no longer is a trip hazard, or make sure that fire alarm works so people can safely get out of the building in the event of a fire.

Top Tip: On the subject of trip hazards, slipping on ice and snow can be a serious issue to deal with to not only stop any harm to people and vehicles but reduce the come-back on anywhere-there's-a-blame-there's-a-claim type of insurance claims. On any external surface you're responsible for, you'll need to show how you're managing this—signage, putting down grit, snow clearance, or actually clarifying that someone else, maybe the end occupier, has to do these themselves and say providing a grit bin with shovel for this.

The people process side is then how people operate at the property and is more to do with people and occupier issues, although with some bearing on property issues. So if they don't have many staff or visitors there, the occupier tenant may need to look more closely into Lone Worker issues and measures like others checking up on them and emergency mobile phone contact as non-property process issues, as well as property issues such as good locks on the doors.

The trick with all of these is to work with the people assessing all these risks as most issues should boil down to common-sense solutions that can be agreed upon and then implemented. Just issuing a standard off-the-shelf risk assessment may look impressive but may not stand up if any incident needed close investigation, as evidence will be required that this relates to real life at the property.

Top Tip: Smoking at a property can raise health and safety as well as fire issues and was effectively banned in enclosed workspaces (including internal common areas in flats) and public areas (with some exceptions) from 2007. In your home, you may be able to, but if this is let, then check the lease as to whether it's allowed, as landlords often don't allow it in order to save the smell and stains inside the property and reduce the risk of fires. Generally, it's not permitted within inside shared area of properties, which leaves the outside areas, although generally away from buildings to reduce risks. This can bring other challenges though, such as spacious and costly smoking shelters and whether provisions are made for people to leave cigarette butts.

RIDDOR

RIDDOR is an abbreviation of Reporting of Injuries, Diseases, and Dangerous Occurrences Regulations 2013 concerning how certain serious accidents, occupational diseases, and certain dangerous occurrences (near misses) are reported and dealt with. It's a duty affecting employers, self-employed, and 'responsible persons' in control of work premises.

So as well as the usual processes for dealing with such injuries, such as first aid help, accident-book reporting, and calling emergency services and help, this is an obligation to contact the relevant authority to inform them about it by the 'quickest possible means', ideally online, but this can also be calling the Incident Contact centre for both reporting and advice.

Landlord Focus: Clarify what you're responsible for, which may still be parts of the areas actually demised to the tenant, particularly with residential properties. Having a good risk assessment carried out by a responsible person will help.

Investor Focus: You need to have any liabilities clarified and sorted so it can't come back and bite, particularly when authorities like insurers or even mortgage lenders ask these questions. The emphasis here is more the documentation of these, not just the initial risk assessment but action points from this.

Tenant Focus: It's essential to sort out what you and your landlord is responsible for and if there is any cross over as the way you use the property may affect the landlord's issues and vice versa.

45. Fire Regulations

Key Points: This is a huge area but with similar principles to the Health & Safety issues. Here are the things to consider:

- *The principles*
- *Practical v. processes*
- *Emergency lighting*

The Principles

The principles within the area of fire-compliance in properties are the same as general Health & Safety; in fact, fire issues are one of the main aspects of general Health & Safety issues. There are also specific pieces of legislation to consider, such as the Housing Act 2004 for inside some residential properties and the Regulatory Reform (Fire Safety) Order 2005 for common areas, which, although aimed primarily at workplaces, does apply to residential properties with common parts and Homes in Multiple Occupation (HMO).

There will need to be a 'responsible person' who takes charge of this, maybe the landlord or, if a direct liability under the lease, a tenant, or through a managing agent for a communal shared area. Years ago the emphasis used to be more on other authorises like the Fire Authority and Fire Certificates being issued, whereas now this 'responsible person' needs to take charge, with services like the Fire Service only tending to offer help and advice afterwards, not do the job for the responsible person.

This person, then, needs to carry out a Fire Risk Assessment using similar principles as a general Health & Safety one by looking at potential issues and risks at a property and actions to try to reduce or eliminate them but specifically focused on fire issues. This includes a suitable Fire Safety Strategy and looking at risks to relevant people, which may include visitors and other tenants.

In terms of the whole gist of this, the idea is to first minimise the risk of fire even starting at a property, and secondly, if one does occur, then quickly and effectively informing people on site to leave as soon as possible with as little hindrance as possible. People quite rightly are the priority here, not the property—let the building burn down if it means people getting out safely first.

Top Tip: If there are any notable changes and alterations to the property, particularly with internal layouts, then you may need to not only update the Fire Risk Assessment but seek building control consent for building fire-detection and prevention measures. There may also be additional changes to the building fabric needed; for example, converting former office buildings into residential units can mean fire-stopping requirements, which is basically filling holes and gaps between areas of the building to stop smoke spreading.

Practical v. Processes

Similar to Health & Safety, there first tends to be property-specific issues to deal with. So look at what systems there are to first detect a fire—fire-alarm system, smoke detectors—and how they are linked to each other if a multi-let building. They can also be monitored, so a monitoring company receives a signal when it goes off and arranges the fire service to site; otherwise, it's a case of people calling 999 themselves.

Top Tip: For residential property, there needs to be careful consideration of what's needed. Check out things like the Local Government Association (LGA) LACORS Housing Fire Safety guidance, and for HMOs and with communal areas, the Department for Communities & Local Government (DCLG) Fire Safety risk assessment.

A recent change is now the requirement for smoke alarms in all private residential lets on each story of the property where there is a room used wholly or partly as living accommodation, although with no specific alarm types within this obligation, so it can include standalone battery ones (ideally long-life batteries). Make sure these are then checked at the start of any tenancy and then periodically afterwards by the landlord or as agreed, say on a monthly basis, by the tenant (see similar provisions for carbon monoxide detectors).

Then look at procedures for escape, which can include both practical and people issues. Look at fire-doors being there and closed so that fires don't spread quickly and the escape routes being kept clutter-free so people can easily get out of the building. You can also have fire extinguishers to help fight fire, although these are less important now than what you may think and are only there for worst-case scenarios.

In terms of getting out of the building, there may need to be a Fire Assembly Point outside for people to congregate at, with a designated Fire Marshall to take control and make sure everyone is present. Lifts generally shouldn't be used as well, and people need to know where the actual fire exits are in the building if anything does happen.

Top Tip: You'll need to carefully consider security issues at the property, which can, at first glance, be opposite to fire issues. So a door leading out of the building on one side needs to always be able to be opened out to leave in the event of an emergency but on the other side may have to be kept locked to stop people from getting back into the building day to day.

Emergency Lighting

This is an unusual requirment in that it really relates to fire issues but it is an electrical item to practically consider. The idea is that if there was a power cut or maybe the fire alarm activation, then lights come on in the main escape routes for people to see how to get out of the building. These are powered by back-up batteries in the lights or separately in the building so that you can guarantee they will always be lit irrespective of a power source.

In terms of checking, they tend to need monthly flick tests to make sure they still operate okay on battery power and an annual discharge test to basically flatten the batteries to make sure they're still okay if lit for longer periods of time.

Landlord Focus: You'll need to get involved with this somehow, even if it's all the tenant's responsibility; you'll need to check that they have it correctly covered, particularly with the building items working properly.

Investor Focus: This is another liability you need to have clarified with correct assessments and action points, and be particularly aware of how these may need to link with any alterations to the property.

Tenant Focus: Even if your landlord is responsible for all this with, say, residential short-term lets, make sure they have it covered and that you know what to actually do in the event of an emergency. Watch out for things like burnt toast accidently setting the smoke detectors off, and don't be tempted to disconnect just for convenience.

46. Gas Safety

Key Points: Gas safety is important, with legislation detailing how it should be carefully managed. Here are the main issues:

- *The residential duty*
- *The commercial duty*
- *Carbon monoxide*
- *Pro- and reactive action*

The Residential Duty

Under the Gas Safety (Installation and Use) Regulations 1998, landlords of residential properties are responsible for gas appliances, fittings, and flues being safe for tenants. On one side, if you're planning to make any changes and alterations to the building, you'll need to check compliance through a qualified plumber and gas installer—issues like what can be fitted in bathrooms and kitchens, using instantaneous water heaters, and any issues of flues and ventilation.

The other big side to this is that residential landlords have a statutory duty to arrange an annual Gas Safety Check by a Gas Safe Registered Engineer. These popular 'gas safety checks' are needed every year in order to check everything over and issue a certificate, with a copy sent to the tenant upon occupation or within 28 days of the check and the landlord keeping a copy for two years.

Top Tip: A landlord's obligation for an annual gas safety checks also includes portable gas appliances like LPG gas heaters popular in residential properties. Tenants that supply or inherit them should still be having them checked anyway, and check that they are permitted by insurers and landlords.

The Commercial Duty

There is no such black-and-white legislation regarding commercial business property, although similar to residential, there is a general common-law duty for gas installations and appliances to of course be safe. The key, then, will be the lease as the landlord could discharge this to the tenant and include it within their demise and liability to carry this out, whereas residential landlords of short-term lets have certain duties they cannot get away from.

There is also a new area of compliance beginning through the Heat Network (Metering & Billing) Regulations 2014, which affects any provisions of heating, cooling, and hot water on a shared communal basis in a building, including wider non-gas ones as well. It applies to the heat supplier, often the landlord, who is in charge of this shared system, for example, the same central heating system in a block of flats or offices.

The emphasis is to make sure energy isn't wasted in such a system and that each individual occupier has information and control over its careful use. Billing must be accurate based on actual reads and data, which could override any set contributions in a lease. Heat suppliers must inform the relevant regulatory body about the communal heating systems, and viability assessments will be needed in due course.

Carbon Monoxide

With residential property, carbon monoxide alarms are needed in any rooms wholly or partly used as living accommodation that contains a solid fuel-burning combustion appliance (already needed with new installations under building regulations). Similar to the requirement for smoke alarms earlier on, these can be standalone battery ones (ideally long-life batteries), and make sure these are then checked at the start of any tenancy and then periodically afterwards directly by the landlord or any agreed say monthly basis by the tenant.

Pro- and Reactive Action

So firstly, be proactive and check who's responsible for gas installs and equipment through the law and the lease. They then need to get things correctly checked over at least annually, even with commercial property ideally, and keep records correctly. If you're making any changes, get this checked out in regards to any implications for gas installs and appliances.

Secondly, be ready to correctly react if there was ever a problem. Educate occupiers to know how to leave the property and turn anything off at the cut-off valve, and then contact the National Gas Emergency Service, available 24/7, to help respond. You can often smell gas, which should always be detected; an example may be an outside gas pipe that a vehicle has accidently crashed into or a problem with the system inside the property.

Top Tip: Make sure the gas meter is easily accessible and that any consumption charges are based upon actual reads.

Landlord Focus: For residential property, you have a definite duty to fulfil, although similar action is advised for commercial property as well. Make sure your tenants are clued up on what to do in the event of an emergency and that they're not doing anything to affect gas issues.

Investor Focus: In addition to evidence of any basic compliance, make sure the gas appliances have been fully checked to detect any long-term issues that may need dealing with.

Tenant Focus: Clarify whether it's you or your landlord who needs to check things, and then make sure you know how to react to any issues.

47. Disabled Persons

Key Points: Those involved with property may have a duty to cater for disabled persons, so here are the key points to consider:

- *The service provider*
- *The principles*

The Service Provider

The core pieces of applicable legislation are the Disability Discrimination Act 1995 and, more recently, the Equality Act 2010. There are also additional duties with management of residential properties under the Disability Discrimination Act 2005. The emphasis is on a 'service provider' (i.e., someone who is providing a service) who quite understandably has to make reasonable adjustments to assist disabled people.

With property, this can be a variety of people depending on who is providing the service—maybe the tenant occupiers or the landlord themselves for shared communal areas. It can therefore be a mix of people, hence the importance of formally asking others if they also have any considerations in a building to be aware of in order to consider how these issues will affect and overlap each other.

It can also be related to reality, in that you may have tenants in a building who have no immediate disabled persons on their staff or contractors or potential visitors to the property, and the requirement on them and the landlord will be low. But if they employ a new staff member who needs wheelchair access, then that tenant will need to make adjustments to their area and inform the landlord to consider for the shared areas.

There is also a greater emphasis on newer legislation for those providing services to the public, and to be more proactive in anticipating the needs of disabled people generally rather than waiting until a particular person requests an adjustment.

There are three other points here as well—firstly, there can be a general duty within, say, building control, so, for example, in a new extension, there may automatically have to be a disabled toilet installed according to the regulations, irrespective of what actual service provider is using them now.

Secondly, if you're a tenant with a lease that restricts you making suitable alterations, this legislation can override it by insisting that your landlord does provide permission on a reasonable basis, although this doesn't include other third parties, like those benefiting from land covenants or the planning authority.

Thirdly, this is just looking at it from a property perspective, whereas an organisation that employs people will have their own obligations as an employer as well.

The Principles

It boils down to making reasonable adjustments for disabled persons. Ideally, changes to the property are needed, but they're not necessarily essential if other common-sense solutions can be applied. So with a disabled person in a wheelchair, although the textbook answer would be to have new doorways, toilets, and ramps installed so they can easily manoeuvre around the property, you could come up with another solution. Maybe the occupier makes employment changes for flexible working or even using other premises, or their workstation could be in an area of the office that is more easily accessible. There could be a temporary ramp or chairlift available to use at key times, and arrangements could be made for them to use the disabled toilet in adjoining areas.

Also remember that the range of disabilities can be wide. So for those who have a visual impairment, then maybe focus on using bright colours and letters or signs to be easily seen. Or if there are learning difficulties, then provisions for them to have separate training facilities on site.

Ideally this should all be assessed in an audit of the whole of the property. This can then pick up obvious property issues, such as disabled toilets and access ways, lifts for wheelchair use, and even handrails on stairs being correct. Make sure you think of common sense, and think long term.

Top Tip: Remember to consider the principle of disabled person when looking at the fire-escape issues in a building as well. So in the event of a fire and people needing to exit the building, disabled persons can actually be encouraged to stay on the premises as other persons leave first or to utilise an evacuation chair provided as lifts should not be used in this eventuality, or there could be special refuge areas to remain in.

Landlord Focus: A lot will depend upon the actual type of use and occupation of the property, so formally request details from each service provider and tenant, and then think through common-sense solutions that affect both yours and the tenant's areas.

Investor Focus: Make sure this has at least been addressed to see if it is applicable in any Health & Safety Risk Assessment or if, ideally, a separate Disability Access Audit being carried out.

Tenant Focus: As a user of property, consider this both now and in the future, including potential visitors. Be prepared to discuss sensible solutions with the landlord rather that assuming that the building fabric can be automatically changed, although if it does and your landlord is causing hindrances, there are procedures for you to formally request this irrespective of the lease, as long as they are reasonable.

48. Electricity Regulations

Key Points: This is an important aspect of properties in order to be safe and compliant. Here are the main issues:

- *The obligations*
- *The practice*

The Obligations

The common misunderstanding here is that there must be formal regular inspections and maintenance, similar to gas. Although there isn't direct legislation like with gas appliances and supply, there is an indirect obligation in two other ways.

The first is by various other legislation, basically implying that the electrics must be 'safe'. This makes sense when dealing with electricity and the potential harm it can cause to property and people. As well as a general common-law duty of care and building regulations for any electrical works to comply with, you have legislation like the Landlord & Tenant Act 1985, Housing Health & Safety Rating System under the Housing Act 2004, Electrical Equipment (Safety) Regulations 1994, the Consumer Protection Act 1987, and Plugs and Sockets etc. (Safety) Regulations 1994.

This focuses on residential property; however, with commercial property and HMOs, there is a statutory duty under the Regulatory Reform Fire Safety Order 2005 for a responsible person to carry out a Fire Risk Assessment, which includes electrical safety risks.

Secondly, there can be other specific obligations, two classic ones being a specific clause in the lease saying that electrics need checking and also with the building insurance that a certain type of inspection is needed by a certain qualified electrician. The other, of course, is through building regulations for any new or major works.

The Practice

So in terms of what's needed, think of this in three stages. Firstly, a proper and full inspection on a regular basis. Even if this isn't a black-and-white requirement in a set time frame, you need to easily demonstrate that things are safe; otherwise, if there was a problem, you would have no defence.

You'll need a qualified electrician, ideally every year with residential property and certainly within 10 years of a new install and every five years thereafter; plus, you can come across what is known as a five-year hard or fixed-wire test with commercial properties, which basically includes a thorough check of all electrical circuits in a property.

Secondly, do and record a basic visual inspection on a regular basis, ideally every year, or when there is a change in the property, for example, a new tenant. Record what's there and any potential problem using a set checklist if you want.

Thirdly, carry out a PAT test on portable appliances if needed. This is a separate issue, really, and has to do with any loose items like kettles or equipment that separately plug into a socket. Again, this is not a strict requirement but really needed to show that things are 'safe'. It is more applicable for users of the building unless property owners or landlords have these already in tenant or communal areas.

Top Tip: Also consider electrical compliance with any alterations, fit-outs, or major works. As well as making sure they are the correct specification, make sure they are completed by qualified electricians and in line with regulations, such as the latest edition of Part P of the Building Regulations with residential property and the Institution of Engineering & Technology (IET) Wiring Regulations.

Landlord Focus: you'll need to be involved with this in most cases, unless, say, it's a commercial property where the whole property and electrics are demised to the tenant with an obligation for them to do this. In this case, though, it's worth chasing the tenant to show that they have and are doing this by making the relevant clauses in the lease as specific as possible.

Investor Focus: You really need a current, up-to-date, full report on the electrics as this can identify what the long-term as well as immediate needs are. Also check any other requirement from your insurers or even funders.

Tenant Focus: Check what you're responsible for and that this is both fair and actually permitted by law. So with short-term residential lots, a landlord has obligations for the main electrics that they can't pass on to the tenant. Check both your contents and the landlord's building insurance policy for any requirements, and also see if PAT applies for your appliances.

49. Asbestos

Key Points: Asbestos is often misunderstood, the severity of it underestimated, and the way it must be dealt with overrated. Here are the main issues to be aware of:

- *When it applies*
- *Asbestos surveys and management plan*
- *Immediate and potential actions*

When It Applies

Asbestos was banned from any building works from February 1999 onwards, but properties before this may contain materials with asbestos in it, originally chosen for qualities such as strength and fire-resistance in buildings. The Control of Asbestos at Work Regulations 2002, with associated codes of practice and guidance, now shapes how asbestos is detected and managed in older buildings due to the effects on people's health it is now understood to have. If these asbestos particles are inhaled by people, they can cause various asbestos-related illnesses, hence once the health impacts of asbestos were understood, it was then banned.

Therefore, if your building was built prior to 2000, then this affects you; if not, then it doesn't—often solicitors will still request a standard 'asbestos report' in a sale or letting, but you can simply say it's not applicable if post 2000.

Asbestos Surveys and Management Plan

You need to have an Asbestos Survey carried out to determine if it is actually present in your property. There are specialist surveyors who can inspect and take samples, and they have to make assumptions that asbestos may be in materials if there are any uncertainties or limited access. Popular areas include roof and wall panels, floor tiles and covering, and old textured wall coverings.

You will then need to determine an Asbestos Management Plan through a qualified person, and review on a regular basis. It's basically a plan of action on how to deal with any asbestos issues in your building following the general survey and is often missed by people that assume that the initial survey is enough. This is something that must then be available and communicated to all related people at the property, particularly any kind of contractor or builder at the property who need to confirm in writing that they have seen, noted, and actioned anything appropriate.

Immediate and Potential Actions

From this Asbestos Management Plan, you'll need to check for any immediate and urgent actions needed. In the majority of cases, nothing is needed other than labels on materials that do or may contain asbestos in order to warn others. The classic misunderstanding is that asbestos in your building is the problem when in actual fact it's not—it's only when it's moved or tampered with that you have issues; otherwise, it can stay where it is.

If you do need to tamper with any asbestos material, then this can only be done by special licenced contractors. This will be dictated by the survey and management plan, with urgent matters to be removed or made safe, or if you are carrying out any future repairs or refurbishment that will mean disturbing asbestos materials. Even simply drilling a hole in a wall with asbestos plaster will require a specialist contractor to deal with it so that they carefully remove any dust, etc.

Landlord Focus: You need written confirmation that you have these measures in place, including the survey and management plan and how you're communicating to any contractors or others as well as appropriate actions being taken. Check the lease with any tenant as it technically may fall within their remit to carry this out in their area; however, practically, it may be worth you arranging for the whole building and maintaining control and then maybe see what element of the costs can be recharged to tenants.

Investor Focus: Check that these are in existence and correct in any existing properties or any new ones being purchased. This is a legal requirement, and it can throw up all kinds of actions and remedial works that will have an effect on your costs for the property. This can be a classic problem that slows down or stops any sale or letting from going through.

Tenant Focus: Check if this is your responsibility through your lease. Even if it is, it may be worth discussing with your landlord to come to an arrangement as to who carries this out within your demise and the rest of the building, and if it is the landlord's responsibility, then request this from them as you'll need this information in order to know how to deal with issues within your area, to appoint contractors, etc.

50. Water Systems

Key Points: *Water systems and supply at a property have different angles to consider:*

- *Basic supply and disposal*
- *Flooding*
- *Water systems*

Basic Supply and Disposal

In short, suss out how water comes into the property and then how it is removed. See where the pipes are, water stop-taps to turn off, any water meters, how the drains operate both for normal water and then sewerage/foul from toilets, and storm drains outside the property for when it rains and ends up in gullies and drains. There will be a mixture of these things both inside and outside the property, which will somehow interlink with adjacent properties and then mains supplies and networks.

This is important information that needs to be reflected in the paperwork, whether it's a lease or the actual ownership title. Clarify who is responsible for these parts, particularly with bits that exclusively serve an area that may be outside the main area/demise. Clarify how you are going to resolve issues and any problems, for example, blocked drains.

Gullies and gutters may not be able to cope with the degree of rainfall and can cause flooding, or neighbouring land can emit things that they shouldn't into the drains. For example, a takeaway retail shop that puts grease down the drains—a common problem—can cause blockages; things like grease-traps may need looking into as well as reactive clearance costs.

Top Tip: It's often helpful to understand the true situation with sewers, drains, manholes, and gullies, both on your own property and neighbouring or communal/highways land. Try to establish plans and routes, see if there is any existing drain survey or if one is possible (you can even run small CCTV cameras along these to determine condition and blockages), and find out from basic drain clears or by asking others if there are any problems, particularly when it rains.

There is also the role of your local water authority to consider and what parts they are responsible for. This has changed over the years, and you need to check whether any communal points both on and off the land are under their liability and what they will help resolve. This can create problems and expenses, so even though they may be responsible and therefore maintain any communal supply through your property, you will need to seek their permission for any proposed building works near them and connection to, including any of their upfront costs for the supply survey.

Top Tip: Also check any water bills you receive to make sure that these are correct. I was once involved in an industrial estate next to a canal where it came to light that the storm water went straight into the canal rather than the water supplier's main run, hence they not only agreed to reduce charges going forward but a large payment was sent back to reflect overcharges over the years. You may also find that your property has been given the wrong banding which can then be adjusted.

Flooding

Although these don't occur every day, when they do happen, they can cause serious property damage and insurance claims. You can therefore have flooding surveys carried out in an area to see if they are prone to this if they're near local rivers for example, and see what the history is in the local area.

Check if your mortgage company or insurance is going to have requirements for this if there is a problem, and see what practical measures you may need to carry out.

Water Systems

Actual water systems, pipes, and equipment at a property must be both properly maintained and looked after in order to reduce the risk of issues like legionnaires disease, which is a potentially fatal form of pneumonia caused from inhaling small droplets of contaminated water with Legionella bacteria. There is a responsibility to therefore manage these correctly and safely under general legislation like the Health & Safety at Work etc. Act 1974 and specific ones like the Control of Legionella Bacteria in Water Systems (L8).

Recently, there has been new specific legal obligations to have a legionnaires disease risk assessment, even for private rented residential properties; however, there are standard templates and guides around for a landlord or agent to do this themselves on straightforward domestic hot water systems for example, with low risks and insignificant control measures without having to bring in consultants and excessive measures such as water testing and samples.

So first see who is responsible for this as a responsible person, and then look at assessing the risks and issues involved. These can be referred to in a general Health & Safety Risk Assessment, or you can have specific Water Risk Assessments completed to go into more detail, advisable even if it's a simple situation. This shows you've made an assessment and that you're doing all you can to make things safe.

Secondly, understand what practical issues exist. Check if there are potential leaks, and if the systems need upgrading, or are there lots of 'dead-legs' in the pipework that need removing. Also get a record of what's there and where important things like meters and stop taps are at the property.

Thirdly, make sure you are using the water systems correctly to minimise issues and the risk of legionella bacteria. So one area to consider is that hot water is always hot enough and cold water cold enough, with monthly temperature tests of running water often needed, and practical things like not changing your hot water boiler or hot water system so it gets below a certain temperature and to spot any problem like lukewarm or discoloured water and hot water that is not coming out hot enough.

Another area is to stop water stagnation, so keep taps and showers running every week for a few minutes and weekly flush-test records, and when a property is reoccupied, as well as cleaning and de-scaling shower heads every few months. There can be chlorination tests of water storage tanks and even sampling and testing of water to make sure everything is okay.

Top Tip: Check whether you need to turn the water supply off at a property for a while, for example, when vacant for the insurers, over the winter to stop the unused system from freezing and risking bursts, or to stop the risk of electric water heaters bursting and being undetected. Also make sure there are not even small water leaks that are causing highs water bills, so monitor bills based upon actual use.

Landlord Focus: Get on top of what you have and then who's going to do what in order to maintain things. This applies even more with vacant properties, and it may be a requirement of your insurance.

Investor Focus: See if there is a water risk assessment that goes into more detail about the condition of the water systems here and any others like drain or building surveys as well as details of the water systems. This will help you discover any hidden issues and potential costs.

Tenant Focus: Clarify what you're responsible for, which may involve liaising with your landlord in order to understand what systems exist and how to look after them best. Watch out for vacant periods as you will still need checks in place, and look at turning things off.

51. Lifts

Key Points: *This is a specialised area not always applicable, but where it is, here's what to consider:*

- *Basic legislation*
- *Insurer's requirements*
- *Maintenance*
- *Procedures*

Basic Legislation

One of the main pieces of legislation governing the maintenance and safety of lifts is the Lifting Operations and Lifting Equipment Regulations (LOLER), which applies to passenger lifts. The gist is that a lift has to be checked periodically by a qualified person to make sure things are safe, obviously with lifts and great heights being such a concern. Every six months is often the minimum, with further in depth ones possibly being needed as well.

You'll therefore need specialist advice on this, however clarify what the bottom-line necessity is as there may be lots of good advice and new improvements recommended as well. Also be aware of the different types of lifts that exist; as well as a typical passenger lift in an office or apartment block, there can be goods-lifts, or stair lifts, or small platform lifts.

Top Tip: Remember to consider general risk assessments, fire risk assessments, and disability audits in context of lifts as they can suddenly introduce other issues. Even an asbestos survey will need to carefully inspect the hidden lift shaft, although any detected asbestos here is often okay to just leave if it won't be tampered with.

Insurer's Requirements

On top of basic legislation, your insurance often has certain criteria. You'll probably need special engineering insurance cover just for the lift plant and kit, and they often insist on regular six-month inspections themselves instead of or in addition to the ones due under general legislation to make sure all is well.

Maintenance

Two words of caution here regarding the maintenance of lifts. Firstly, you will need a specialist lift contractor, but be careful how these are selected. Check any contract and what's included in terms of basic services, call outs, dealing with emergencies, and extra charges. Also consult with others like the insurers, a separate LOLER inspector, or even a specialist lift consultant.

Secondly, think long term about what issues could be around the corner. This includes 10 to 20 years ahead, and although it may be all okay now, if it's already 15 years old, then you may start seeing big issues emerging. This may not be as bad as it sounds, as it may just take carefully planned repairs over time.

Procedures

The way in which you run and operate lifts is important. You really need a lift policy taking into account legislation, inspection reports, risk assessments, insurance requirements, and the unique circumstances about the property and how it is used.

Place notices in and around the lift on what to do in the event of an emergency and break down, and check how people raise the alarm. Older lifts tend to have a manual alarm or button that sounds in the building, but someone else needs to be in the building at the same time in order to hear it; in this case, no one should be using the lift when they are alone in the building. Some do have a link through a phone line with, say, BT that sends a signal to a company maintaining the lift to then have a call-out service to resolve.

Make sure everyone knows what to do while they wait for help. If someone is trapped in the lift, then no one should be even trying to get them out other than a lift contractor or fire brigade, although you can have others standing on the other side making sure they are okay until they arrive.

Landlord Focus: In the majority of cases, the buck stops with you, so make sure it's correctly inspected and maintained and that the long-term issues are understand. Then communicate everything to all users of the property.

Investor Focus: Watch out for big costs further down the line and issues from non-compliance now. Sift through any standard reports to get the bottom-line answers and reality.

Tenant Focus: In most cases, this will be your landlord's responsibility, although if it's just serving your area, it could be within your lease responsibilities. If so, and if you have the opportunity, try to exclude this liability back to the landlord. Whoever is responsible, make sure you know the procedure for dealing with, and communicating through to individuals to correctly use.

52. Furniture

Key Points: Having furniture left in a property can mean an obligation to make sure it's safe. Here's what you need to consider:

- *Basic compliance*
- *Clarification and documentation*

Basic Compliance

The basic concern is fire; therefore, for furniture with flammable upholstery, verify that it's not going to cause or encourage any fire at a property. The main piece of legislation is the Furniture & Furnishings (Fire) (Safety) Regulations 1988 along with future amendments and the Consumer Protection Act 1987 for those that first supply these to someone.

This will mainly apply for residential property and holiday lets, the important factor being that there is a suitable label on any new or second-hand items to show compliance.

If you think this applies to you, then search for the detail online, see what items they refer to as it can exclude items such as loose pillows, and make sure you have the correct labelled items.

Think of general safety as well—so no sharp edges and things loose or broken. Even legislation like General Product (Safety) Regulations 1994 can refer to glass in furniture being suitable and lampshades being able to cope with and labelled for whatever bulbs you have.

Clarification and Documentation

Be clear on what's what and who it belongs to. If you're a residential landlord and you're providing it furnished, then it's a straightforward responsibility of yourself; this can be referred to in the lease and inventory or schedule of condition.

But if it isn't formally provided by the landlord, watch out for a new tenant taking items on from an old tenant or a new tenant using old and uncompliant pieces of furniture. Or maybe it starts off being a tenant's item but it becomes fixed to the property and so legally becomes a landlord's fixture.

Keep it simple—clarify who takes it on liability wise, and simply note it and then correctly check, even if just by a letter or email.

Top Tip: Also consider any requirements from your buildings and contents insurance as to what is permitted.

Landlord Focus: As well as clarifying any items that you formally provide as being safe and compliant and recording this, note what a new tenant inherits either from something already in the property or their own items, and check any requirements with insurance policies.

Investor Focus: Check what potential liability you may be carrying, particularly with furnished or holiday lets.

Tenant Focus: Check any items that your landlord has provided and that it has the label on and is safe, and likewise make sure your own items are safe and sound.

53. EPCs

Key Points: Becoming energy efficient and 'greener' with properties is becoming the name of the game, so here's what to consider:

- *The basic gist*
- *Energy Performance Certificates*
- *Minimum energy efficiency*
- *Energy sources*

The Basic Gist

Not only is this a very confusing area to understand with various options and good advice but it's ever-changing as things and ideas evolve. You therefore often need to take a step back and see what is trying to be achieved.

We need to all become greener and energy efficient, whether that's emitting fewer CO2 gases into the environment, using less energy and utilities, or having environmentally sustainable materials. Aside from the whole discussion on whether this is needed or not, the fact remains that countries and governments are set on doing this, with the UK government's statutory commitment to reduce the country's carbon emissions towards 2030 to see a 80% reduction from 1990 levels.

As much as 50% of the UK's carbon emissions are attributable to the construction and operation of properties. Properties are therefore seen as a big factor in this, both their construction and how they're run, so they're in the firing line to become greener whether we like it or not.

Years ago this was a great idea, but it was left to the good intentions of people involved with property to do these things. Now it's starting to make financial sense through market forces and government legislation, therefore it's starting to be a bigger factor in reality.

Top Tip: The government previously introduced the 'Green Deal', where an additional charge is paid via the electricity meter charge over time in order to use Green Deal Finance to fund energy efficiency improvements at a property.

With tenants and leases, it must be clear that they will be paying this under their period of occupation, with a copy of the EPC needing to detail the Green Deal and acknowledgement to pay in the tenancy agreement.

Energy Performance Certificates

One of the biggest-hitting changes in this area to the property market is the provision of an EPC when you sell or let properties, both residential and commercial. The same one can remain for ten years without renewal, but they need to be carried out by a qualified person. The idea is that it provides upfront information for a potential buyer or occupier as to how energy efficient a property is, graded from A to G, and looks at all kinds of factors and building issues in order to calculate this.

There are two practical issues to remember. Firstly, they are centrally lodged, so they can be easily accessed once needed. Secondly, the timing is critical; because they are now a legal requirement, they are needed right at the start of the selling/letting process, not as an afterthought after marketing has begun.

Minimum Energy Efficiency

This is where things spice up. The Minimum Energy Efficiency Standards Regulations (MEES Regulations) are coming into play to insist upon minimum levels of EPC assessments for both residential and commercial properties over the next few years. So from April 2018 under the Energy Efficiency (Private Rental Property) (England & Wales) Regulations 2015, it will be illegal to not only grant a new lease but renew an existing one of a 'substandard' building where the EPC rating is F or G. By April 2023 this will automatically include all leases.

In short, works will be needed to the property to increase the EPC rating in order to become relatable, and therefore this is a serious concern for property owners and occupiers to be looking at now rather than having an unlettable building in 2018. Example works include improved insulation of walls, doors, roofs, and windows. Also the installation of renewable energy sources as well as more efficient heating and cooling and lighting systems, new energy metering, and recommendations from an EPC report.

There is a cap on these, though, so that the cost of these works is still less than the expected energy cost savings. It includes works anyway under a Green Deal plan, and you'll be exempt if third party consents are not possible from a lender, tenant/landlord, or planning authority. There are also some exemptions, such as listed buildings and lettings more than 99 years or under six months, although these exemptions need to be registered and only last five years under the current ownership.

Top Tip: For larger businesses and public sector organisations in the UK, the CRC Energy Efficiency Scheme also applies, which provides an obligation to measure and report on their energy consumption and purchase 'allowances' for the amount of CO_2 emissions associated with that level of consumption. This is a specialised area that will need additional advice.

Energy Sources

The level and type of energy used at a property, namely electricity and gas, will have an increasing impact at a property. There will be pressure to use less, and the cost from the utility providers will increase, hence the need to look at using less through more efficient heating/lighting and looking at alternative sources of energy.

Top Tip: Solar panels on properties are becoming more popular now, and although they can look prominent on the roof, they can not only help reduce/eliminate your electricity costs going forward but you can get paid for sending power back into the national grid. The initial cost can therefore be soon offset by these cost reductions and any initial grants/loans to fund. However do look at options, make sure issues like planning and lease arrangements are clarified, and make sure it is a legitimate scheme and provider.

Landlord Focus: Make sure you not only have a valid EPC now but look into whether this will cause issues in the future and if there are any long-term works you can prepare for now in conjunction with your tenants.

Investor Focus: You need to look at this long-term perspective for your property, maybe having a full energy report by a specialist surveyor to look at options. Also see where funding and support is available, including through occupiers and tenants, and check to see if going green for yourself will pay off in the future, particularly with larger companies and corporations.

Tenant Focus: Check if there is an EPC in place, and see what measures can help you have reduced running costs as well, particularly with lower utility costs because of the landlord doing things like better insulation and more efficient heating systems.

CONCLUSION

The world of property management can be confusing, and half the battle is being able to understand exactly what the real problem is and how to best go about resolving it. This is why I felt there was such a need for this book, something that can help literally guide you through the issues surrounding property management in the UK—something that isn't full of theoretical information but helps broaden people's horizons to see the bigger picture and see just how many issues there really are and how they then relate to each other.

I have often compared it to spinning lots of plates at the same time as an example of how it can sometimes feel when trying to keep lots of things ticking along in order to make sure the end goals of, say, improved rent and capital values, reduced running costs, or just greater satisfaction are all accomplished. This may sound like an impossible task, but once you've learnt the art of doing it, then it becomes surprisingly so much easier.

So as we conclude this Property Management Guide, that is the best piece of advice I can end with: Keep an eye on your end goal and a wide perspective on all of the issues actually involved in achieving that as this will then enable you to go into more detail on whatever subject later on.

If you are say a landlord with tenant arrears or a tenant without funds to pay rent, then you will naturally focus on the black-and-white solution of how to quickly pay or collect the money. Quite rightly this is the end goal, but by looking at the other perspectives, principles, and points within property management, you might deduce a better way to resolve this.

It might involve learning from this current situation and making sure money is paid again or is resolved better, or how best to communicate with other parties for better results, or how to use other sources, such as guarantors and deposits. You might also need to look at the practical property issues that affect this rent and even the bigger picture of this rental income stream continuing in the future.

In terms of remembering how all these different issues then come together, think of it as "benefiting three type of people, through four different perspectives, by fifty three unique principles, and shaped by various points

— all to form the right path". This does sound a bit daunting at first, but it is a concise tagline for the bottom-line guidance in this book.

There is a quick summary at the end of each principle for these three people interest groups that this book is aimed at: landlords, property investors, and tenants. Even if you naturally fall within one of these categories, reading the others will also benefit you in that you will see the issues through another person's perspective.

We then have a total of 53 different principles to consider that cover all the main issues within property management. Within these there are separate points with key points summarised at the top of each principle, and additional top tips included to help add that extra value and advice where possible.

These 53 principles are then grouped into four different perspectives, or rather ways of looking at property management. There is the property perspective and literally looking at the building practically and the issues involved. Then there is the people perspective and considering what individuals and interests are involved. We then have the payments perspective and what monies are involved with those property interests followed by the paperwork perspective and what documentation is often needed to clarify and confirm things.

Once you have gone through these 53 principles and through the four perspectives, you can then start seeing how these all link together for you personally and what the next steps are.

One of the first action points then is to jot down what immediately springs to mind after you have gone through the whole book or whatever sections you needed to. This is particularly helpful if you have a specific query in mind as often things will jump right out as they start making sense; therefore go with what you first instinctively pick up, and write it down. Even if you're seeking to just widen your general understanding of the property management arena, then this act of noting what first comes to mind can still be extremely helpful.

Secondly, know what area you then need to research more. This guide will help you get on track; however, you may need to find more information and specifics on certain issues. This can be both on and offline and by yourself or with other people and organisations helping you out. There is an amazing amount of information available on things nowadays, but the challenge is to know what bits you need and then to make sense of these for your situation.

Thirdly, I'd recommend re-reading the book or certainly specific parts of it, particularly if you want a good grounding in the subject. This will help cement any points you picked up the first time and allow other things to emerge as you go through a second time. It's also worth keeping this book as a reference point for the future, something you can dip into if certain issues crop up later or you're facing a new property interest and need a fresh perspective on things.

And finally, you can find out more helpful information at our website, www. propertymanagementguide.co.uk/bookpurchase, where you can not only see helpful blogs and updates on different subject areas of property management but, as a purchaser of this book, further information to help you out, including paths as a sort of checklist and summary of how to go through the issues one by one for different scenarios. Please also feel free to contact us directly for any advice or further pointers.

In the meantime, wishing you all the best as you start your own unique path through the world of property management.

GLOSSARY

Here is a glossary in alphabetical order of some important terms and phrases within the world of property management and this book. As with the gist of this Property Management Guide, these are not necessarily technical text-book definitions but more a practical interpretation of how they apply to property management.

They also include the most applicable ones along with those you may hear in general terminology within property management which may be more just general reference rather than a technical term.

Accounts Payable – the part of accounting paying Supplier invoices.

Administration Charge – a charge for the processing of an issue or request from one party to another under an agreement, often due at a reasonable level under the agreement or legislation.

Adverse Possession – the right of people occupying property to eventually take ownership of it.

Alienation – transferring a lease interest from one tenant to another often by assignment, subletting or sharing occupation.

Asbestos – a certain material used in older building now known to potentially cause illness to people when disturbed, therefore a legal requirement for those in control of properties to have these first surveyed through as Asbestos Survey, and then a system agreed of removing or controlling through as Asbestos Management Plan.

Assets of Community Value (ACV) – the designation of a building or piece of land as having community value.

Assignment – when the existing lease is transferred to another tenant and therefore changing the tenant's name on the lease.

Assured Shorthold Tenancy (AST) – a short term tenancy often six months long for residential properties entitling the landlord to re-possess afterwards.

Authorised Guarantee Agreement (AGA) – a separate agreement between a former tenant of a commercial lease and a landlord to guarantee a new tenant after an Assignment.

Balance Sheet – an accounting statement of assets and liabilities of a business.

Break Option or Clause – an agreed point in a lease or agreement where it can end early by both or one party giving set notice and possibly meeting certain conditions.

Building Regulations & Control – minimum specifications for any building works prescribed by legislation.

Business Improvement District (BID) – an additional Business Rates charge agreed for a region that goes towards specific services in that area.

Business Rates – a form of occupation tax for business interests.

Capital Allowances – set amounts that a business can deduct from tax on their profits, for example expenditure items on properties.

Cash and Bank Reconciliations – where monies in bank accounts are cross-checked with actual transactions on an accounting system to ensure they are correct.

CDM – an abbreviation to obligations under the Construction (Design & Management) Regulations for larger works needing to have a formalised system of managing health and safety on site as managed by an appointed person.

Commercial Rent Arrears Recovery (CRAR) – the procedure for commercial property landlords to recover rent arrears by notifying the tenant before then looking to cease their goods, replacing the former remedy of distrain through bailiffs.

Commonhold – a new form of ownership for common areas in a residential development introduced in 2002.

Conservation Area – an area designated with environmental importance, and having additional restrictions imposed on the types of changes and works permitted.

Construction Industry Scheme (CIS) – a system of deducting tax from sub-contractor payments where applicable.

Consumer Protection – legislation and regulations around consumers generally including their involvement with properties, for example purchasing new developments.

Contents Insurance – insurance cover for personal items of the occupier and their fittings.

Council Tax – a form of occupation tax for residential dwellings.

Directors and Officers (D&O) Insurance – insurance cover for those as directors and officers of a company.

Disability Discrimination Act – legislation for appropriate people and organisations to provide adequate help for disabled persons accessing their services or properties, which can involve building changes.

Electricity Regulations – requirements under legislation to regularly assess the safety of existing electrical circuits at a property.

Emergency Lights – a system of battery-operated lighting that will automatically come on in the event of a power cut to a building so that people can see their way out of the property.

Employers Liability Insurance – insurance cover for employers against staff and any work-related losses and injuries.

Energy Performance Certificate (EPC) – an assessment required by law for property transactions to summarise the energy efficiency of a property as graded with letters from A to G, with the Minimum Energy Efficiency Standards being introduced to bring in a minimum level.

Enforcement Notice – a notice served by the local authority for a breach in planning law.

Enfranchisement – for residential long lease hold interests the rights of tenants to purchase the freehold of the property individually or as with Collective Enfranchisement on a joint basis with other residential tenants in the same property.

Financial Services Authority (FSA) – an independent body that regulates businesses in the financial services market.

Fire Assembly Point – an agreed point for people to meet outside away from the building if they need to leave the property in the event of a fire or false alarm.

Fire Marshall – an appointed person in a group of people occupying a building to account for and organise people in the event of them needing to leave the premises when there is a real or suspected fire.

Fire Regulations - obligations under regulations for when a building is first built or having major works to have prescribed levels of fire detection and control, but also for responsible persons to regularly reassess this in any property afterwards.

Fire Risk Assessment – a risk assessment specifically referring to risks and issues under Fire Regulations.

Five Year Hard or Fixed Wire Test – with commercial property the recommendation to fully check all electrical circuits every five years, often required by authorities like funders and insurers.

Furniture & Furnishings – reference to the provision of these in properties to let, with some legal obligations for their safety.

Gas Safety Check – legal obligation for short-term residential landlords to have an annual gas safety check of the property.

General Permitted Development Order (or Permitted Development Rights) - where certain works are automatically allowed without needing to apply for planning permission.

Grants – funding provided to a business or interest for the purpose of some greater good, with or without conditions and often with an initial application process.

Green Deal – a former government scheme allowing loans for energy saving measures at a property.

Health & Safety – general reference to considering people's health and safety at properties as under various legislation, and regarding files of information prepared for new buildings and works.

Highways Agency - a government agency responsible for maintaining the network of roads and public highways and walkways in the country.

Human Rights – the rights of individuals through legislation which can have an effect on how properties are managed and transacted, and includes Freedom of Information.

Improvements – when works or alterations to a property are improving the property and its value, often in the context of tenants works under a lease or landlords works through a service charge.

Insolvency – general reference to the financial difficulty or demise of a party, with different forms including Bankruptcy, Administration, Liquidation, Receivership, and Voluntary Agreement.

Insurance Excess – an amount the insured needs to pay towards an insurance pay-out, often a few hundred pounds.

Insurance Revaluation - re-assessing the cost of re-building a property in the event of severe damage, different to the transaction market value.

JCT Minor Work Contract – a standard document for smaller building jobs between the contractor and person instructing.

Land Registry – the government body logging legal land and property ownership and interests.

Law Society – the organisation that sets standards and regulates solicitors.

Lawful Development Certificate – a certificate issued to confirm the legality of a certain use or development.

Lease Extension – often in the context of residential long leaseholds and the right to request lease extensions.

Legionaries Disease – the illness caused from inhaling a certain bacteria that can grow in stagnant and wrong-temperature water, therefore requiring water systems to have regular running water and correct cold and hot temperatures.

Lift – both reference to a provision in a building to move passengers and goods to different floors, but also the Lift cost referred to by businesses removing refuse as to the cost for removing one bin's waste.

Listed Building – designation as a special building meaning that it cannot have certain works or repairs without Listed Building Consent.

LOLER – an abbreviation for legal obligations under the Lifting Operations and Lifting Equipment Regulations to regularly inspect passenger Lifts in properties.

Marriage Value – when a residential long lease holder purchases the freehold and the value paid takes into account the additional value of the interests coming together.

Money Laundering – obligations under legislation for parties to make enquiries and checks to ensure that property transactions are not involving illegal monies.

Mortgage – a legal agreement where a funder releases money to purchase a property in exchange for holding the deeds of the debtor's property as security in case they do not repay in full.

Non-Resident Landlord Tax – for landlords based outside of the UK but receiving an income from a UK property, declaration with HMRC as to whether tax is deducted or not.

Notice to Quit – notice issued by a landlord to a tenant to leave the property under an agreement by a certain time frame.

Party Wall – general reference to a wall between two areas, and more specifically through the Party Wall etc. Act 1996 regarding proposed works to these by one owner and how they need to involve and communicate with other owners benefiting from this.

PAT – an abbreviation for Portable Appliance Testing and the recommendation for every electrical item that is plugged-in to have regular checks.

Periodic Tenancy – a tenancy that continues on a regular basis, for example weekly, monthly, or yearly.

Permit to Work – for higher risk activities and works where a system of allowing these is required after looking at the risks and actions involved.

Pre-Let Lease – a lease agreed to take effect in the future after certain conditions are met, mainly the construction or refurbishment of a property.

Private Rent License – for certain parts of the country, particularly London, where all private residential landlords need a licence from the local authority.

Private Rented Sector (PRS) – where properties are owned for the purpose of short-term residential lets and the benefit of an income stream, currently a developing market.

Professional Indemnity (PI) Insurance – insurance cover for an individual or business against claims of negligence, particularly applicable for external parties.

Profit and Loss – a financial statement summarising the income and expenditure items within a time period, often a year.

Public Liability Insurance – insurance cover for losses and injuries to the general public.

Qualifying Tenant – often referred to in residential long leasehold legislation regarding those with certain rights.

Quarter In Advance – the payment of monies every three months, often with business leases, and paid in advance on the quarter starting rather than in arrears at the end of a quarter. Traditional start dates of these quarters are the 25 March, 24 June, 29 September and 25 December; for Modern Quarter Days they are the 1st January, 1st April, 1st July, and 1st October.

RAMS – short for Risk Assessments and Method Statements, where both these documents are combined into for one ease of use and reference.

Rates Exemptions & Relief – certain scenarios where no or reduced Business Rates are due.

Regulated Tenancies – short-term residential leases granted before 1989 with statutory protection.

Reinstatement – when alterations are removed and the property is re-instated back to the original condition it was in before, sometimes known as Yielding Up.

Relevant Disposal – the point of a landlord selling their interest in a residential property where long leaseholders have a right of consultation and opportunity to purchase.

Reversionary Lease – a completed lease now but beginning in the future, for example to take effect at the end of a current lease.

RIDDOR – an abbreviation of Reporting of Injuries, Diseases, and Dangerous Occurrences Regulations and the need to report any serious injuries to a government-appointed body.

Right to Manage (RTM) – the right of residential long leasehold owners to take over the management of the shared areas from the landlord.

Risk Assessment – a method of looking at potential risks to a property and situation and the possible harm and preventative actions that can result from this.

Section 146 Notice - served under the Law of Property Act 1925 regarding procedures to forfeit a lease because of a tenant's breach.

Section 17 Notice – a notice served to former commercial property tenants to notify them of current-tenant arrears needing payment.

Section 25, 26, and 27 Notices – served under The 1954 Act by landlords or tenants to request a termination or extension of a protected business lease.

Section 8 & 21 – procedures and notices under residential property legislation to deal with short-term tenancy arrears and termination.

Stamp Duty Land Tax (SDLT) – a form of tax on property sales and lettings in set bands.

Subletting – a different tenant taking occupation through an additional sub lease in place under the original main head lease.

Superior Leaseholder or Landlord – the landlord above the immediate one where there are multiple leases in place for example a sub-lease under a head-lease.

Suppliers – the parties who provide a service to a property in exchange for a payment. From an accounting perspective they will generally include all parties paid, but from a practical perspective mainly contractors.

Surrender – when a legal agreement, often a lease, is agreed by both parties to terminate earlier than the original term.

Tax and VAT Returns – the point of submitting details to HMRC of your accounting information for general tax purposes normally every year, or three months for VAT purposes.

Tenancy at Will – a form of agreement between an occupier and owner without full documentation which can be terminated at any time by both parties.

The 1954 Act – referring to legislation called the Landlord and Tenant Act 1954 which is the main piece of legislation regarding commercial property leases with the focus on how they are ended and extended through rights of tenants to continue and 'holding over'.

Town or Village Green (TVG) – ability to designate a communal area of land and protect its use as a town and village green.

TUPE – an abbreviation of rights under the Transfer of Undertakings (Protection of Employment) Regulations where individuals have employment rights to continue even though the main contractor changes.

Use Classes – agreed bands of use that a property can have without needing planning permission, with some movements between bands being permitted without permission.

Valuation – the assessment of a property interest's value, according to various methods of valuation.

Valuation Office – the government organisation who set the levels of Business Rates, in turn charged out by the local authority.

Value Added Tax (VAT) – tax paid on a relevant supply or charge on a service, varying for different properties and parties, and needing a regular return completing to HMRC.

Water Risk Assessment – a specific risk assessment for the water systems at a property for both heating and water supply, to ensure safety and eliminate the possibility of Legionaires Disease.

Work at Height – a specific risk assessment looking at the issues surrounding individuals needing to work or inspect off the ground, for example from ladders.

Printed in Poland
by Amazon Fulfillment
Poland Sp. z o.o., Wrocław